adventures in
HEXAGONS

11 Quilts, 29 Blocks, Unlimited Possibilities

EMILY BRECLAW

C&T PUBLISHING

Publisher: Amy Marson

Creative Director: Gailen Runge

Editor: Lynn Koolish

Technical Editors: Debbie Rodgers and Gailen Runge

Cover/Book Designer: April Mostek

Production Coordinators: Zinnia Heinzmann and Joe Edge

Production Editor: Alice Mace Nakanishi

Illustrator: Freesia Pearson Blizard

Photo Assistants: Carly Jean Marin and Mai Yong Vang

Photography by Diane Pedersen of C&T Publishing, unless otherwise noted

Published by C&T Publishing, Inc., P.O. Box 1456, Lafayette, CA 94549

Library of Congress Cataloging-in-Publication Data

Names: Breclaw, Emily, 1976 author.

Title: Adventures in hexagons : 11 quilts, 29 blocks, unlimited possibilities / Emily Breclaw.

Description: Lafayette, CA : C&T Publishing, Inc., 2017.

Identifiers: LCCN 2016035576 | ISBN 9781617452826 (soft cover)

Subjects: LCSH: Patchwork--Patterns. | Quilting--Patterns. | Hexagons. | Repetitive patterns (Decorative arts)

Classification: LCC TT835 .B692 2017 | DDC 746.46--dc23

LC record available at https://lccn.loc.gov/2016035576

Printed in China

10 9 8 7 6 5 4 3 2 1

dedication

To my parents, Lloyd and Kathy Towers, for teaching me how to reach for the stars, and to my husband, Derrick, for believing I could quilt them.

acknowledgments

This book would not have been possible without the support of so many lovely people. Thank you to Amy Jameson, for the amazing longarm quilting. You rock. Thank you to Elizabeth Simmons, Hillary Shenkle, Trey Towers, Greg and Debbie Breclaw, Cathy Slovensky, and Teresa Duryea Wong for support and encouragement throughout this journey. Thank you to Candice Hoffman, Daryl Cohen, Demetria Hayward, and Stephanie Menjivar for providing gorgeous fabric. Thank you to all the online friends and followers of The Caffeinated Quilter—your kind words and interest in my work mean the world to me. And thank you especially to my five wonderful children. Thanks for putting up with my craziness, making me smile even on deadline days, and reminding me of what's most important.

Contents

PROJECTS

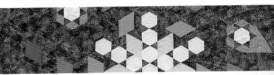

Introduction

Hexagons make stupendous quilts. Their unusual shape, ability to tile, and radial patterns are inspiring. Intricate hexagon quilts merit a second glance at a quilt show, and they beg the question, "How did the quilter do that?"

Adventures in Hexagons answers that question. In the following chapters, you'll find several detailed methods for cutting and piecing hexagons. Whatever method you choose, you'll soon discover that hexagons aren't really any more difficult to sew than squares—and they're considerably more interesting!

Traditionally hexagon quilts have been considered a one-patch layout, meaning hexagons of the same shape and size are used across the entire quilt (think Grandmother's Flower Garden and Tumbling Blocks). With *Adventures in Hexagons*, you can stretch the boundaries of that one-patch grid and use it as a springboard for creating designs with multiple sizes of hexagons in one quilt.

Here's how it works: Think of a *block* in terms of how many hexagons are used to create it.

A **single block** is made up of one hexagon.

A **triple block** is made up of three hexagons, giving you the freedom to incorporate a more complex design than you can with just singles.

A **rosette block** is made up of seven hexagons (six surrounding a single center hexagon). This is the same hexagon arrangement as you would find in a Grandmother's Flower Garden quilt, but by playing with how you fit shapes within that seven-block arrangement, you can create a large variety of designs.

The final two block types you'll explore in this book are sprockets and medallions.

Sprockets are made up of thirteen hexagons. Think of them as rosettes with extra hexagons around the edges. The uneven edge of this shape gives your quilts a dynamic impact.

Medallions are the showstoppers. With nineteen hexagons combined into this super-rosette shape, you have a lot of room to incorporate all kinds of 60° shapes into visually stunning designs.

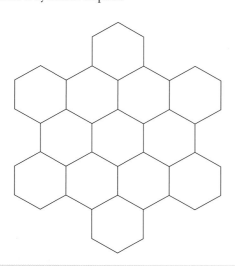

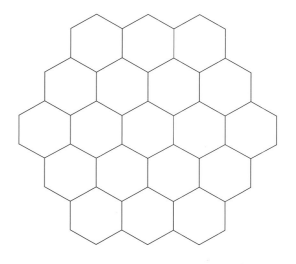

They still fit within the one-patch layout but allow for designs much larger than the original hexagon.

Combine all of these together and you have a hexagon sampler quilt that is truly stellar.

Adventures in Hexagons presents a framework illustrating the use of the hexagon grid as a tool for creating unusual layouts and radical (radial) designs that defy tradition.

Mini-quilts made by Emily Breclaw featuring Chalk and Paint fabrics, by Sew Caroline for Art Gallery Fabrics

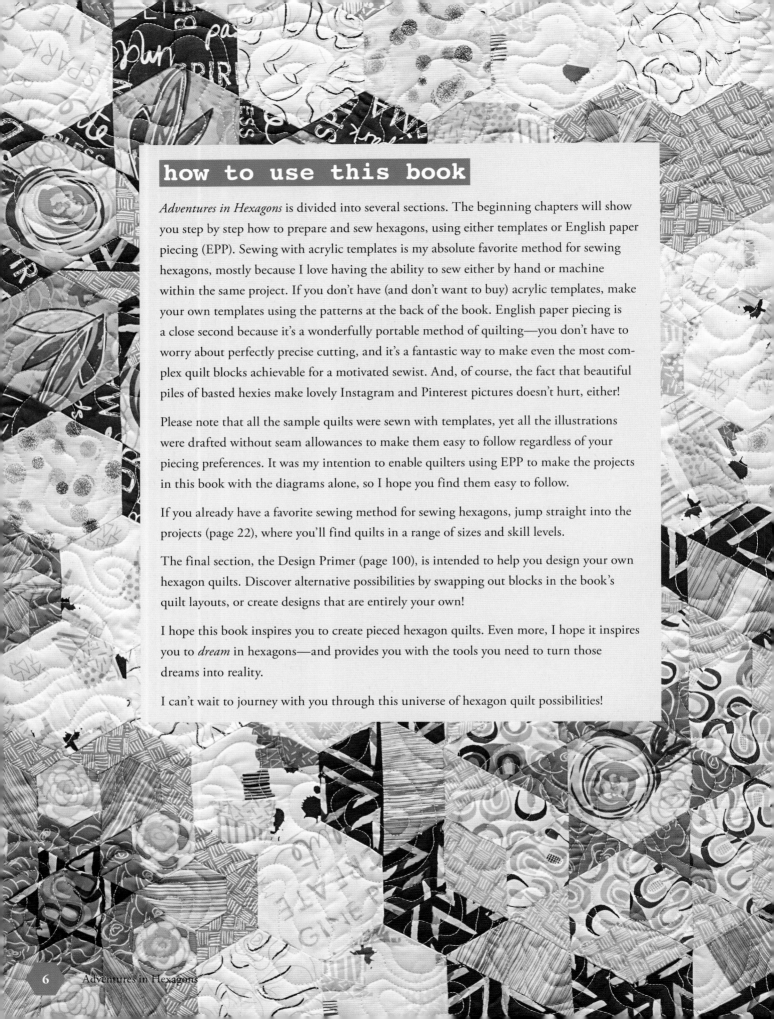

how to use this book

Adventures in Hexagons is divided into several sections. The beginning chapters will show you step by step how to prepare and sew hexagons, using either templates or English paper piecing (EPP). Sewing with acrylic templates is my absolute favorite method for sewing hexagons, mostly because I love having the ability to sew either by hand or machine within the same project. If you don't have (and don't want to buy) acrylic templates, make your own templates using the patterns at the back of the book. English paper piecing is a close second because it's a wonderfully portable method of quilting—you don't have to worry about perfectly precise cutting, and it's a fantastic way to make even the most complex quilt blocks achievable for a motivated sewist. And, of course, the fact that beautiful piles of basted hexies make lovely Instagram and Pinterest pictures doesn't hurt, either!

Please note that all the sample quilts were sewn with templates, yet all the illustrations were drafted without seam allowances to make them easy to follow regardless of your piecing preferences. It was my intention to enable quilters using EPP to make the projects in this book with the diagrams alone, so I hope you find them easy to follow.

If you already have a favorite sewing method for sewing hexagons, jump straight into the projects (page 22), where you'll find quilts in a range of sizes and skill levels.

The final section, the Design Primer (page 100), is intended to help you design your own hexagon quilts. Discover alternative possibilities by swapping out blocks in the book's quilt layouts, or create designs that are entirely your own!

I hope this book inspires you to create pieced hexagon quilts. Even more, I hope it inspires you to *dream* in hexagons—and provides you with the tools you need to turn those dreams into reality.

I can't wait to journey with you through this universe of hexagon quilt possibilities!

Cutting and Preparing Patches

Using acrylic templates and English paper piecing are my two favorite methods of sewing hexagon quilts. Although you cannot use both methods in the same quilt, each is useful in particular situations. Acrylic templates are fantastic to use with large quilts, especially since you can sew them easily by machine. English paper piecing is probably the easier of the two methods to learn, and it is a great starting point for your hexagon journey.

Before starting any hexagon quilt, regardless of the method you choose to use, you need to understand how hexagons are measured. Looking at templates in a quilt store can be confusing, because different manufacturers label hexagons with differing measurements. Some measure hexagons through the middle side to side, some measure through the middle point to point, and some measure along the length of a single side.

Templates measured through the middle are convenient for one-patch quilts because the templates are usually made to fit standard strip widths. However, these templates may become confusing in quilts that combine multiple shapes, such as the quilts in this book. For example, a 2″ hexagon measured through the middle cannot be sewn to a 2″ triangle measured through the middle.

important note

Throughout this book, hexagon measurements will indicate the length of a side of the shape, so a 3″ hexagon fits with a 3″ triangle, a 3″ diamond, and so on. A 3″ kite technically doesn't have a 3″ side; when six kites are combined, however, they create a 3″ hexagon. This is also the way most die-cutting companies measure hexagons, so every quilt in this book can be made using either English paper piecing or templates.

However, a 2″ hexagon measured along a side fits perfectly with a 2″ triangle measured along a side.

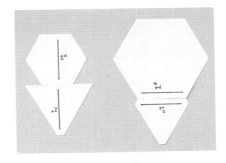

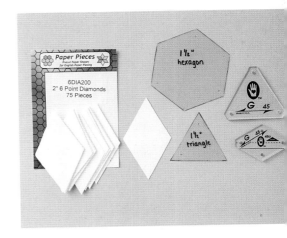

For the projects in this book, you may purchase precut paper pieces (I like paperpieces.com) or acrylic templates (frommarti.com is a good source), or you may make your own. Patterns for all the shapes in this book are included in Patterns (page 105).

making templates

To make your own templates, trace the patterns in the book onto template plastic and cut them out carefully. I highly recommend marking a dot at each point of the shape sewing line (inner lines) and, using a $\frac{1}{16}''$ hole punch, punching a hole at the dot you drew so you can mark the dots where your seams start and stop.

You can also use the pattern pages to make your own paper pieces for EPP. Just trace around the inner shape (sewing line) for your paper pieces.

TIP If you like the idea of template sewing but not the idea of marking patches, you may want to check out Inklingo (inklingo.com). Through this website you can purchase PDF files of various shapes and print the cutting and sewing lines directly onto the back of your fabric. Inklingo shapes are also measured along a side (see Important Note, page 7), so they are compatible with most of the projects in this book.

cutting fabric for template sewing

Tools

• Rotary cutter

• Rotary mat and ruler

• Templates

• Pencil

• Rotating cutting mat (not essential, but a lifesaver when you're cutting lots of shapes)

Cutting Shapes from Strips

The cutting list for each project includes the number of strips to cut for each shape.

1. Cut the strips to the indicated size.

2. Place your template along the strip so that the top and bottom edges match the cut sides.

3. Cut the right side of the shape.

4. Turn the strip around (or use a rotating cutting mat) and cut out the other side.

5. Move the cut patch aside and cut the second shape in the same manner as the first. Either line up the template along the previously cut line or leave a tiny edge of fabric so you can make fresh cuts around all sides of the second shape. Either method works well, but the second method is a little more accurate. All measurements in this book account for the small amount of fabric wasted using this method.

If you are cutting many shapes from a strip, you can fold it in half or in fourths before cutting out the shapes to cut multiple patches simultaneously.

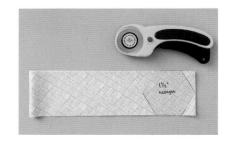

For shapes such as triangles and half-hexagons, turn the template 180° after cutting each shape for less fabric waste.

Cutting Shapes from Pieced Strips

Some projects in this book use shapes created from pieced strips, such as diamonds and triangles. For these shapes, first piece the strips or rectangles as indicated in the project.

For pieced diamonds, place the strips right sides together and sew a ¼" seam along *both* long sides of the strip. Then align the diamond template over the sewn strip and cut.

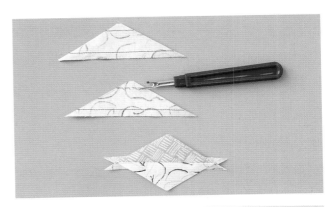

For pieced triangles, sew together the rectangles (right sides together) along one long side and press open. Line up the template so the seamline exactly intersects the triangle point and cut along the template.

After cutting, you will have a half-diamond shape with a seam along the center of the diamond and a tiny section of seam at the wide-angle points. Remove the stitches from this tiny section of seam so you can press the unit open. As an added bonus, you don't need to mark those points, as your ¼" mark will align with the tiny holes left in the fabric from the removed stitches!

Marking Patches for Sewing

After you have cut out your shapes for a project, flip them over to the wrong side of the fabric. Place your template on top of the shape and use a mechanical pencil to mark the dots for each seam start and end point. *Note: You can also use a washout pencil or pen for this step if you are worried about the marks coming out of the fabric later.* I've never had the pencil lead show through on the front, and I find it much easier to fit a mechanical pencil into the tiny holes.

Eventually you may find that you do not need to mark every single shape before sewing them together. For example, in the Starry Singles used throughout this book, I have found it adequate to mark only the triangles.

Note: Fabric requirements given throughout this book err on the generous side. If you are using English paper piecing (EPP) and like to cut your patches with a seam allowance greater than ¼″ around the edges, you may want to consider adding an ⅛ yard to your fabric calculations. If you sew with a ¼″ or a scant ¼″ allowance, you should be fine with the measurements as stated.

Tools and Supplies

• Card stock paper *or* precut paper pieces in the sizes called for in the individual patterns

• Rotary cutter

• Rotary mat

Patterns for all the patches in this book appear in Patterns (page 105). You can copy them onto card stock paper to create your own paper templates. As a general rule of thumb, you'll probably want at least half as many paper templates as the number of shapes in the quilt. You will be able to remove them as you stitch, but you will need to leave some paper templates in the outer edges of your block until they are sewn together. I highly recommend purchasing precut paper templates. They are reusable, accurate, and allow you to spend more time sewing than cutting paper. All the shapes used in this book are common shapes readily available from several companies specializing in EPP, such as paperpieces.com.

Cutting Shapes from Strips

All the patterns in this book instruct you to cut fabric into strips first and then into shapes. When you are cutting hexagons from a strip, you can simply cut the strips into squares, one for each hexagon needed. The photos in Basting (pages 11–14) show how to fold the squares of fabric over a paper hexagon. Cutting squares is faster than cutting hexagons, and the tiny bit of extra fabric basted into a shape does not significantly increase quilt bulk. But if you prefer to cut your hexies exactly, just use the following directions for other shapes.

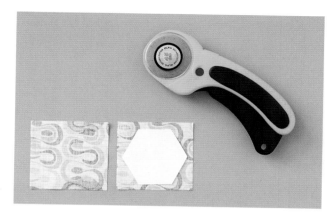

For all other shapes, place a paper template onto your cut strip. Center it roughly ¼″ from the top and bottom of the strip. Using a rotary cutter, cut the sides of the shape about ¼″ away from the paper. (Remember that this will all be folded over and basted, so absolute precision is not necessary here.) For a shape such as a triangle or half-hexagon, flip over the paper shape onto the strip and cut the next piece. Continue until you have the quantity listed in the directions.

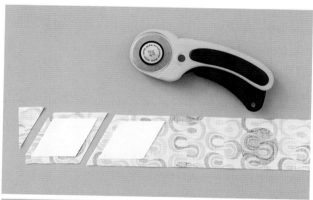

basting

There are several popular methods of basting, and each has distinct advantages. Try out all three of the following methods (You could even test them all in the same quilt—no one will ever know!) and see which one you prefer.

Method 1: Thread Basting through the Paper

This method is an incredibly secure and accurate way to baste hexagons. Essentially you are sewing each side of the shape to the paper. Therefore, your hexagons will not come unbasted before you want them to. Even if you set the project aside for a couple of years, the patches will be just as secure when you come back to it as the day you set it aside. On the downside, this method also wears out your paper pieces most quickly. I can typically reuse papers only twice with this method. (If you gently iron your papers between projects, it helps.) You also must remove your basting stitches at the end of your project, as they show on the front of your sewing.

1. Place a paper template on the *wrong* side of the fabric. Use a thread that does not match your fabric for basting—contrasting thread will make it easier

to see and remove your basting stitches later.

2. Fold over the top edge of the fabric. Bring your threaded needle up from the right side of the fabric (do *not* knot thread). Leaving about a 1″ thread tail, take a small stitch through the paper, fabric, and seam allowance.

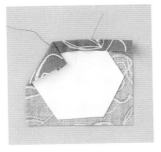

3. Fold over the next side of the fabric, making sure your corner is crisp and folded precisely. Take a small stitch through the paper and all layers of fabric at the corner and

another stitch between the corners.

4. Continue folding and stitching around each side until you return to where you started.

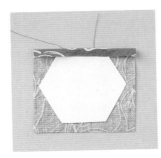

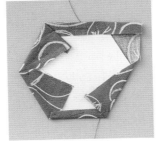

5. Make sure the thread leaves the completed hexagon on the front of the fabric for easier removal.

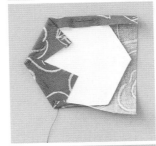

6. Leaving about 2″ of thread, begin on your next piece. It is not necessary to cut your thread between shapes unless they get tangled—think of it as chain basting. The added benefit of leaving pieces attached in this way is that it is an easy method of keeping patches for a particular block organized. You will, of course, need to trim the basting thread between the patches before sewing them together.

Method 2: Thread Basting Without Going through the Paper

If you hate the idea of removing all your basting stitches, this method is a good alternative. It also helps preserve your paper templates for multiple uses. The process to get corners secured accurately is a little more finicky, and occasionally you may find that the papers pop out when you're folding patches to line up seams. Here's how you thread baste without piercing the paper:

1. Place a paper template on the *wrong* side of the fabric. Use a thread that matches or is *lighter* than your fabric. Darker thread could show through to the front once you remove the papers.

Note: Darker thread is used in these photographs for visibility.

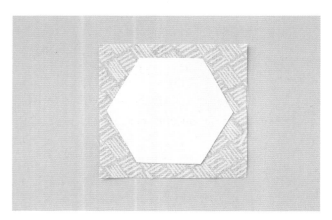

2. Fold over the first and second sides of the patch, and hold the corner securely. Bring your needle through the corner fabrics, leaving a 1″ thread tail and avoiding poking your needle through the paper. Repeat the stitch to secure the corner.

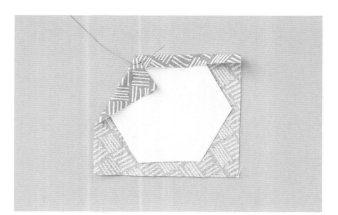

3. Fold over the third side of the fabric, and secure the second corner in the same manner as the first.

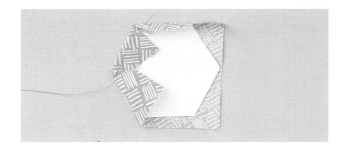

4. Continue all the way around your shape, until all corners are secure. Leave a 2″ thread tail and proceed to the next patch to baste.

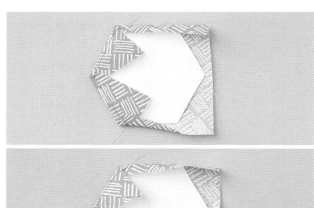

Method 3: Glue Basting

This method of basting addresses some of the issues with thread basting and can be incredibly fast. Just as it sounds, glue basting means you glue your fabric edges to the paper pieces. Pressing the fabric onto the glue gives you very accurate edges to sew along. It takes *much* less time to glue baste a patch than to thread baste it. The method also has some downsides, however. It's worthwhile to purchase special glue pens made for basting, because they make the process significantly less messy and enable you to place a small, fine line of glue along the sides. If you're glue basting a large quilt, you will probably go through many glue sticks, which can get expensive. If you're working on a very long-term project, glue basting may not be your best option, because the glue will degrade over time. But for quick projects, glue basting makes it super easy to get to the fun of stitching quickly. The process is essentially the same as thread basting.

TIP If you live somewhere hot, like Texas, never leave your basting kit in the car in the summertime. Melted glue sticks are depressing. Don't ask me how I know!

1. Place a paper template on the *wrong* side of the fabric.

2. Draw a thin line of glue along the top edge of the paper piece. Try not to get the glue right on the edge of the paper, as that's where your needle will be going through when sewing patches together.

3. Fold the top edge of fabric down over the glue line and press with your finger to help the fabric stick to the glue.

4. Place a thin line of glue along the next paper side, and fold the fabric over the glue line, pressing with your finger to secure.

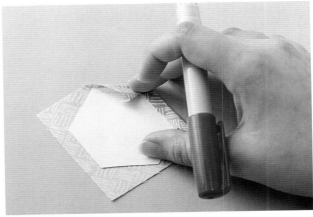

5. Continue around the patch until all sides are secure.

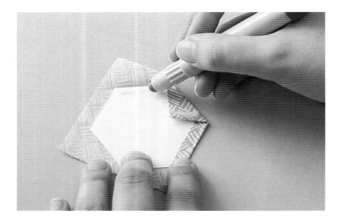

6. Allow the glue to dry before sewing the shapes together.

Basting Shapes with Acute Angles

Not all shapes baste smoothly with all the fabric tucked behind the paper. Shapes such as triangles and diamonds will have little corners (also known as *dog-ears*) that stick out beyond the paper. *Don't cut these off.* They will get tucked behind other patches as you sew and can be invaluable as a visual guide to your points when you're lining up patches to sew.

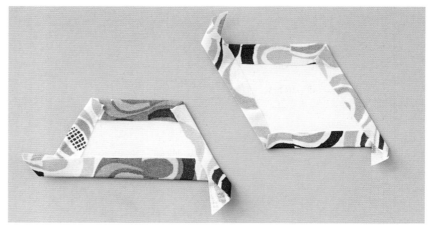

Sewing Hexagons and Related Shapes

sewing hexagons cut from templates

Hexagons can be sewn either by hand or machine, and each method has advantages. Try a few blocks entirely by hand and a few entirely by machine to get a sense of how you prefer to sew them. I tend to switch between methods, using hand sewing for Y-seams and projects with small hexagons. You can even combine methods in the same quilt—as long as you sew from dot to dot, your seams will be accurate.

important note

Whether you sew by hand or machine, the following sections show you how to sew from dot to dot. The dots are the marks you made on the back of your patches when cutting them out; see Marking Patches for Sewing (page 9). Sewing dot to dot is different from piecing straight seams (which allows you to sew from one edge of the patch all the way to the other edge), because you need the flexibility to pivot or turn in the seam allowances.

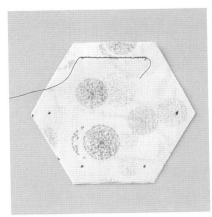

Seam sewn from dot to dot

Hand Sewing

Note: The following photographs use contrasting thread to make the knots and stitches easier to see. Use thread that matches your fabric to keep your stitches inconspicuous.

Place two patches right sides together along the sides you want to sew together. Follow the steps of Making a Knot (page 16) to secure the beginning and end of each seam. Use a running stitch along the seamline until you reach the second seam dot. Go back over your last stitch and knot. Trim your thread close to the knot.

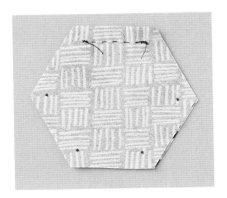

ADVANTAGES OF HAND SEWING	Patches can be sewn continuously without having to cut the thread between adjacent seams
	Portable
	Very easy to pivot seam allowances on Y-seams
	Good for small patches (1½″ shapes and smaller)

ADVANTAGES OF MACHINE SEWING	Faster for chain piecing many units
	¼″ seam foot helps keep seams straight
	Good for large patches and for sewing together rows

MAKING A KNOT

Use the following steps to secure the beginning and end of each seam.

1. Insert the needle at the seam dot, making sure it passes through the dot on the back patch as well. Take a tiny running stitch along the imaginary line between the two seam dots and hold on to the thread tail to prevent it from passing through the hole.

2. Now pass the needle through the same stitch again, and hold the needle in the fabric.

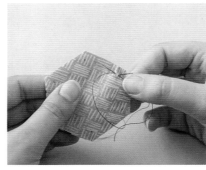

3. Wrap the thread coming from the stitch over and behind the needle, making sure the thread passes behind the needle.

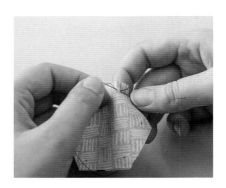

4. Take the end of the thread coming from the eye of the needle and bring it to the tip of the needle. Wrap it over and behind the needle.

5. Now pull the needle through the stitch, forming a small knot in the first stitch.

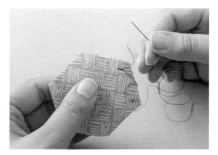

Finished knot

SEWING Y-SEAMS

Sewing Y-seams by hand is simple.

1. After you have sewn two patches together, place the third patch right sides together with one of the patches it will be sewn to.

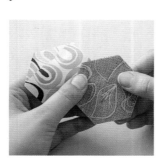

2. Sew the seam with the third patch, as explained in Hand Sewing (page 15); this seam will end at the seam connecting the first two patches. Knot the thread but do not trim the thread.

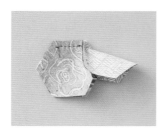

3. Align the third patch to the second, pulling gently to move the first patch out of the way, and sew from dot to dot, knotting the thread at both ends.

4. Trim the thread after finishing the seam. You've completed a Y-seam!

Machine Sewing

Place two patches right sides together along the sides you want to sew together. Pin if desired, and sew. Be sure to lock each and every seam at the beginning and the end. I prefer to lock seams by sewing a few tiny stitches at the start, then switching to a normal stitch length for most of the seam, and switching again to the short stitch for the last few stitches.

TIP On some sewing machines, you can program separate stitches in the memory to accommodate short and normal stitch length. Then you only need to press a button to switch between the two.

You also can lock your seams by backstitching or using the lock-stitch on your machine. These methods are not quite as accurate at the end of seams, as it's much easier to stop exactly on the dot when your needle is moving in small increments. However you choose to do it, be sure to secure every seam at the beginning and end so that you don't end up with seams unraveling and holes in your quilt.

SEWING Y-SEAMS

Sewing Y-seams by machine takes a few steps.

1. Remove the pair of patches sewn with a straight seam from the machine. Clip the threads and open up the two patches.

2. Align the next patch with the next side to be sewn.

3. Sew the straight seam, lock threads, and remove the unit from the machine.

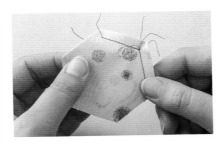

4. Line up the second side of the third patch with the second side of the second patch. Pull the first patch gently to make sure it is not caught in the beginning of the next seam—the first patch will fold in half as you pull it out of the way.

5. Sew the third patch to the second.

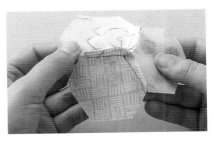

TIP When sewing together rows, the steps are exactly the same as described for sewing patches together (see Sewing Y-Seams, above). With blocks such as the ones in *Sparkler* (page 45), however, you will often wind up with a seam from the block at the corners. This creates a lot of bulk when sewing rows together, and it can be difficult to move that bulk to sew accurately. I have found that pinning *from the back* keeps the seams out of the way and prevents those extra seam allowances from getting caught on the feed dogs and sewn into the seam.

Pressing Units

While you sew blocks together, finger-press the seams out of your way. This is one of the advantages of sewing dot to dot: You don't need to worry about seam allowances getting locked down by other seams crossing them.

When pressing, keep these tips in mind:

• Depending on whether your hexagon layout has the hexagons oriented point up or flat side up, you will have vertical or horizontal seams where the blocks are sewn into rows. Make a habit of *always* pressing vertical seams to the right and horizontal seams up.

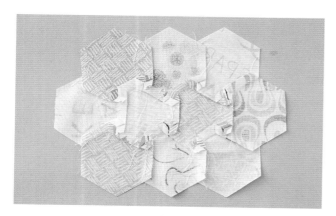

Then swirl the seams around the vertical or horizontal seams. When this is done correctly, the fabric at the intersection will make a tiny hexagon, or Tumbling Block.

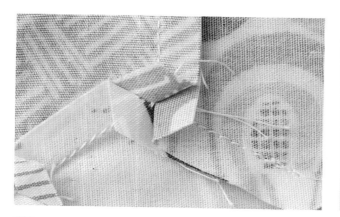

• When pressing a unit (especially a bigger unit such as a rosette), always start in the center. If the center is a hexagon, press the sides of the hexagon in alternating directions.

• Some shapes, such as triangles, don't lend themselves well to these tips. I typically press two sides of a triangle in the same direction to keep things simpler. The rosette below has many triangles interspersed with the other shapes, and in each case, I pressed them however worked best for the shapes around them.

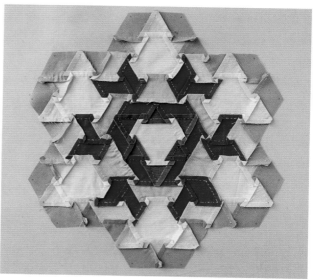

Troubleshooting Sewn Hexagons

Occasionally you may find that when you're sewing shapes, especially in the Y-seams, that the patches don't pivot or turn freely, or that they pivot or turn too freely. Once pressed, the seam may have a small pucker or hole. No worries—these problems are quick to fix and tend to diminish with practice. Following are a few common errors and the simplest ways to fix them.

OVERSTITCHING

Overstitching happens when you stitch past the dot and into a seam allowance. This will prevent your patches from pivoting or turning cleanly. Look at your work from the front side. If you can see a tiny stitch, or pucker in the middle of the Y-seam, you have an overstitch to remove.

If you've machine pieced and used my favorite method of taking tiny stitches as you end a seam, you can simply use a seam ripper to pick out the stitch or two causing the problem.

If you're hand sewing, you will probably need to remove the seam where the overstitch occurred. Typically, however, you'll notice an overstitch as it happens, as you will suddenly find your needle struggling to pierce more layers of fabric than it should be piercing.

HOLES IN THE SEAM INTERSECTION

Holes in your seam intersection are the opposite of overstitching. They mean you haven't quite sewn to the dot.

Look at your work from the back side, folding over each seam to look at it carefully. You'll probably see where you didn't quite get to the end of the seam. Pull any other seams out of the way and stitch to the dot, using the shorter stitch length.

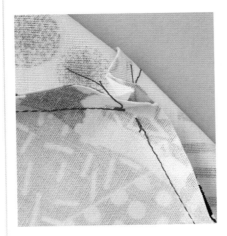

You can also fix the hole by hand by circling the seam intersection. Take a

threaded needle with a small knot at the end of the thread. Hold the piece up so that all the seams around the hole are facing you. Take the needle and go between each seam allowance in a clockwise manner, essentially gathering the fabric around the hole from the back side.

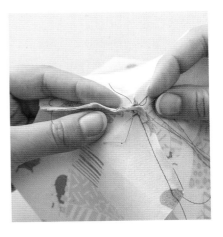

When you get to the knot where you started, pull the thread gently to close the hole. Take a tiny stitch in the seam allowance, and pass your needle through that stitch a couple of times to secure it. Double-check your work from the front to make sure you closed up the hole. Then trim your thread.

You've got all your patches basted and you're ready to sew! This is one of my favorite parts of EPP—at this stage, you can arrange all your pieces for a block, or even for the whole project, and see how it's going to look. How cool is that?

Sewing Straight Seams

When you sew together patches, use a thread that matches the darker patch, as this way your stitches will be less noticeable if they happen to show.

Before joining two pieces, knot the thread. You can form a simple knot by taking your threaded needle, bringing the end of the thread to the tip of the needle, wrapping the end twice around the needle, and pulling the needle through the loops. Hold on to the loops until the knot is at the end of the thread.

1. Begin by placing the two patches you want to join right sides together, aligning the two edges to be joined.

2. Bring the needle up between the folded fabric and the paper to come out exactly at the corner of one shape. Then go through the matching corner of the second shape.

3. Pull gently until the knot is firmly inside the corner seam allowance. Now take a second stitch about 1/16″ past the first stitch, going through the second shape, then the first. Make sure your needle goes straight through both patches, catching only a few threads in the fold of each shape.

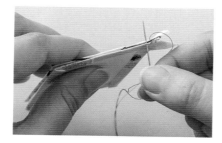

4. Continue taking tiny whipstitches, aiming for about 10 stitches per inch. Your line of stitching should resemble a spiral binding on a notebook.

5. At the end of *every* seam, take a couple of anchoring stitches by doing the following: As you take your second-to-last stitch, leave a small loop of thread temporarily. Pass your needle through this loop twice, going from right to left each time. Then pull the loop tight against the seam. Repeat this anchoring stitch in the exact final corner of the shape.

6. If you are trimming the thread, bury the thread tail by passing your needle through the seam allowance and then pulling gently on the thread and cutting it close to the fabric.

7. When the seam is sewn, open the seam by opening the patches like a book, with the seam as a hinge.

Sewing Y-Seams— Pivoting

One of the beauties of EPP is that it gives you the ability to pivot and continue sewing seams without having to break the thread. If you have a third patch to sew at the hinge of a straight seam, open your two previously sewn patches and align the third patch to sew.

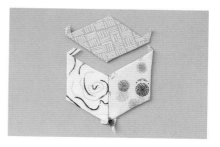

Anchor the stitching to start the seam. Sew the first side of the green diamond to the dotted diamond, and anchor your stitching at the end of the seam. Align the green diamond to the white diamond. Then take a *tiny* backstitch into the folded shape from the previous seam. This prevents holes from forming between patches.

Then continue sewing, just as you did for the previous seam.

Removing Papers and Pressing

Depending on your basting method (and the number of paper pieces you have on hand for a project), you will probably remove some of the piecing papers before you finish your project. Be sure to remove papers only where the patch is completely surrounded by seams. I like to press the front and back of the block before I remove any papers, as that helps to set the seam allowances and keep things neat. I also press again from the front after I've taken out the papers.

If you've basted with thread through the papers, use a needle to help pick out the basting stitches from the back side of the project. If you thread basted without going through the paper, you can bend the patch slightly to make the paper pop out. If you glue basted, gently peel the seam allowances off the paper and pull the paper out. Be wary of areas where you may have used too much glue. Pulling too hard can distort the patch.

sewing borders

1. Fold your quilt in half horizontally and vertically. Press lightly to mark the center of each side.

2. Measure the quilt horizontally (lines A, B, C). Calculate (A+B+C)/3 = top and bottom border length.

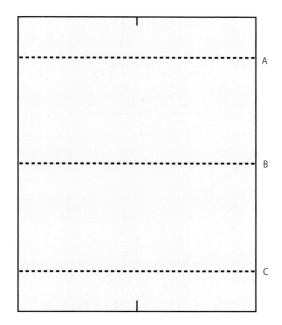

3. Cut and piece the border strips as needed from the project to the exact length calculated in Step 2. Sew them to the top and bottom of the quilt. Press toward the borders.

4. Measure the quilt vertically (lines D, E, F). Calculate (D+E+F)/3 = side border length.

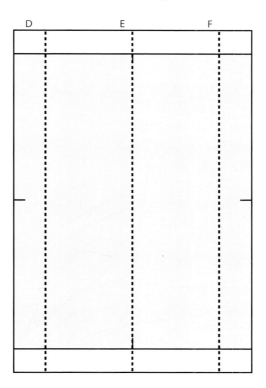

5. Cut and piece the border strips as needed for the project to the exact length calculated in Step 4 and sew them to the sides of quilt. Press the seam allowances toward the borders.

6. You can also measure and add the side borders before the top and bottom borders, as I did for *Confetti in Times Square* (page 38) and *Starburst* (page 53).

Loverly

HEXAGON SIZE: 2″ • FINISHED QUILT: 39¾″ × 15½″

MADE BY
Emily Breclaw

This sweet and simple table runner is a perfect introduction to English paper piecing or a quick project with templates. Use this project to explore piecing triple and single units. Multiple sizes of hearts and layered motifs add whimsy and dimension to the quilt.

materials

DARK PINK: ¾ yard

LIGHT PINK: ⅓ yard

WHITE: ⅛ yard

BLUE: ⅛ yard

BORDER: ¼ yard

BACKING: 1¼ yards

BINDING: ⅓ yard

BATTING: 44″ × 20″

cutting

Use the 2″ hexagon family patterns (pages 108 and 109). In the instructions that follow, large shapes measure 2″ on a side and small shapes measure 1″ on a side. Refer to Cutting and Preparing Patches (page 7) as needed.

DARK PINK

- Cut 2 strips 4″ × width of fabric; subcut into 14 large hexagons.
- Cut 3 strips 2½″ × width of fabric; subcut into 22 large house half-hexagons.
- Cut 1 strip 2¼″ × width of fabric; subcut into 3 large half-hexagons and 8 large diamonds.
- Cut 2 strips 1⅜″ × width of fabric; subcut into 14 small diamonds, 4 small half-hexagons, and 4 small triangles.

LIGHT PINK

- Cut 1 strip 4″ × width of fabric; subcut into 6 large hexagons.
- Cut 1 strip 2¼″ × width of fabric; subcut into 4 large diamonds.
- Cut 1 strip 1⅜″ × width of fabric; subcut into 7 small diamonds, 2 small triangles, and 2 small half-hexagons.

WHITE

- Cut 1 strip 1⅜″ × width of fabric; subcut into 18 small diamonds.

BLUE

- Cut 1 strip 2¼″ × width of fabric; subcut into 6 small jewels.

BORDERS

- Cut 3 strips 2″ × width of fabric.

BINDING

- Cut 3 strips 2½″ × width of fabric.

construction

Seam allowances are ¼″. Do not sew into the seam allowances.
Refer to Sewing Hexagons and Related Shapes (page 15) as needed.

Block Assembly

BIG HEART TRIPLE

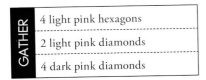

GATHER	4 light pink hexagons
	2 light pink diamonds
	4 dark pink diamonds

1. Sew 2 dark pink diamonds and 1 light pink diamond into a Tumbling Block.

2. Sew 2 light pink hexagons together.

3. Join the Tumbling Block to the sewn light pink hexagons, making sure the Tumbling Block is oriented in such a way that you sew the light pink diamond sides to the hexagons.

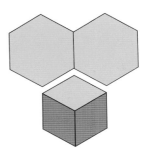

4. Repeat Steps 1–3 to make a second Big Heart Triple.

BABY HEART SINGLE

GATHER	
	4 small blue jewels
	2 small dark pink diamonds
	4 small dark pink triangles
	4 small dark pink half-hexagons

1. Sew a small dark pink triangle to a small dark pink half-hexagon. Sew another small dark pink triangle to a second dark pink half-hexagon, making sure you sew the opposite short side of the hexagon from the first pair.

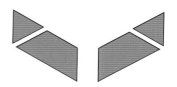

2. Sew a small blue jewel to each of the units from Step 1. You will make mirror-image units in this step, *not* identical units.

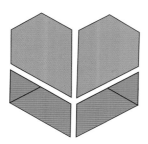

3. Sew the two units from Step 2 together.

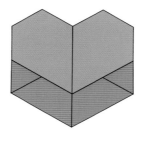

4. Sew the dark pink diamond to the top of the heart.

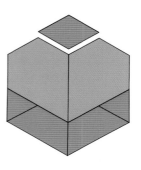

5. Repeat Steps 1–4 to make a second Baby Heart Single.

DIAMOND STAR SINGLE

GATHER	
	12 small dark pink diamonds
	12 small white diamonds

1. Sew 2 white diamonds and one dark pink diamond into a Tumbling Block. Repeat to make a total of 3 Tumbling Blocks.

Make 3.

2. Sew together the white sides of the Tumbling Blocks from Step 1 to create a star.

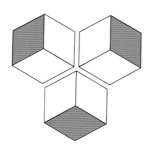

3. Sew 3 small dark pink diamonds to the remaining sides of the unit from Step 2.

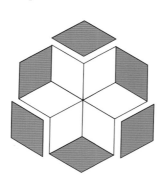

4. Repeat Steps 1–3 to make a second Diamond Star Single.

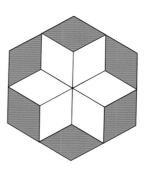

BIG HEART TRIPLE VARIANTS

Create a layered effect by substituting Baby Heart Singles or Diamond Star Singles for the plain pink hexagons in the Big Heart Triple.

GATHER		
6 small light pink diamonds	1 large light pink diamond	
6 small white diamonds	2 large dark pink diamonds	
1 large light pink hexagon		

GATHER		
2 small blue jewels	1 large light pink hexagon	
1 small light pink diamond	1 large light pink diamond	
2 small light pink triangles	2 large dark pink diamonds	
2 small light pink half-hexagons		

Use the small pink and white diamonds to make a Diamond Star Single (previous page). Then follow the instructions for the Big Heart Triple (page 23) to complete the unit, but use the Diamond Star Single in place of the pink hexagon on the left.

Make a Baby Heart Single (previous page). Follow the instructions for Big Heart Triple (page 23) to complete the unit, but use the Baby Heart Single in place of the pink hexagon on the right.

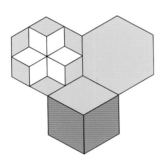

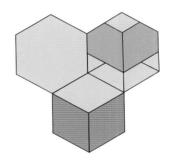

Quilt Assembly

Refer to the quilt layout diagram (page 26) while assembling the rows. Press the vertical seams to the right. Swirl the horizontal seams clockwise around the vertical seams. (See Pressing Units, page 18.)

1. Sew 11 dark pink house half-hexagons into a row. Repeat to make a second row.

Make 2.

2. Arrange and sew the triples, singles, dark pink hexagons, and dark pink half-hexagons into the quilt center as shown.

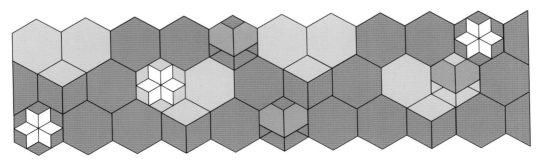

3. Sew the rows from Step 1 to the top and bottom of the quilt. Each will have one half of a house half-hexagon left over. Trim these flush with the quilt sides after attaching the rows.

Borders

Gather the border strips. Refer to Sewing Borders (page 21) to attach the borders to the quilt.

Finishing

1. Layer the quilt top with the batting and backing. Baste and quilt as desired. The quilt as shown (page 22) was quilted with a meandering curlicue pattern.

2. Bind the quilt with the binding strips.

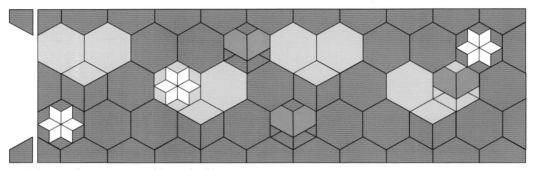

Quilt layout, showing trimmed house half-hexagons

Independence Day

HEXAGON SIZE: 3″ • FINISHED QUILT: 76″ × 91¼″ (twin-size)

PIECED BY Emily Breclaw
QUILTED BY Amy Jameson

Fabrics: Basically Patrick by Patrick Lose for RJR Fabrics

Perfect for a picnic blanket or dorm-room spread, this patriotic quilt goes together quickly with chain-pieced units. The entire quilt is made of super-size medallion blocks with plain hexagons as filler.

materials

BLUE: Scraps or yardage to total 3 yards. (The quilt shown uses ½ yard each of 6 blue fabrics.)

RED: Scraps or yardage to total 2⅜ yards. (The quilt shown uses ½ yard each of 3 red fabrics and ⅞ yard of 1 red fabric.)

WHITE: Scraps or yardage to total 3¼ yards. (The quilt shown uses ½ yard each of 4 white fabrics and ⅝ yard of 2 white fabrics.)

BORDERS: ⅞ yard

BACKING: 6⅞ yards

BINDING: ⅞ yard

BATTING: 82″ × 98″

cutting

Use the 3″ hexagon family of patterns (pages 105–107). In the instructions that follow, large shapes measure 3″ on a side and small shapes measure 1½″ on a side. Refer to Cutting and Preparing Patches (page 7) as needed.

BLUE

- Cut 14 strips 5¾″ × width of fabric; subcut into 82 large hexagons.
- Cut 4 strips 3⅛″ × width of fabric; subcut into 72 large triangles.
- Cut 3 strips 1¹³⁄₁₆″ × width of fabric; subcut into 72 small triangles.

RED

- Cut 4 strips 5¾″ × width of fabric; subcut into 22 large hexagons.
- Cut 18 strips 3⅛″ × width of fabric; subcut into 144 large triangles and 72 large half-hexagons.

WHITE

- Cut 16 strips 5¾″ × width of fabric; subcut into 90 large hexagons.
- Cut 2 strips 3⅛″ × width of fabric; subcut into 12 small hexagons.
- Cut 5 strips 1¹³⁄₁₆″ × width of fabric; subcut into 72 small diamonds.

BORDERS

- Cut 9 strips 3″ × width of fabric.

BINDING

- Cut 10 strips 2½″ × width of fabric.

construction

Seam allowances are ¼″. Do not sew into the seam allowances unless otherwise noted. Refer to Sewing Hexagons and Related Shapes (page 15) as needed.

Block Assembly

STAR-SPANGLED MEDALLION

FOR EACH MEDALLION, GATHER:	
	1 small white hexagon
	6 small blue triangles
	6 small white diamonds
	6 large blue hexagons
	6 large blue triangles
	6 large white hexagons
	12 large red triangles
	6 red half-hexagons

1. Sew 6 small blue triangles to the small white hexagon.

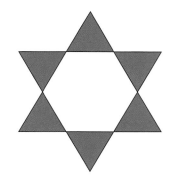

2. Sew 6 small white diamonds around the blue triangles to create a pieced star.

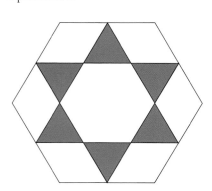

3. Sew a large blue triangle to a large blue hexagon. Repeat Steps 1–3 to make a total of 6 large jewels. *Fig. A*

A

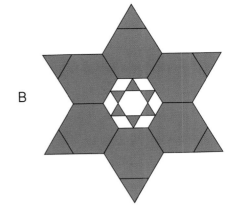

B

4. Sew the jewel shapes around the pieced star from Step 2. *Fig. B*

5. Sew 2 large red triangles to opposite sides of a large white hexagon. Repeat to make a total of 6 pieced diamonds. *Fig. C*

6. Sew the pieced diamonds to the unit from Step 4. *Fig. D*

C

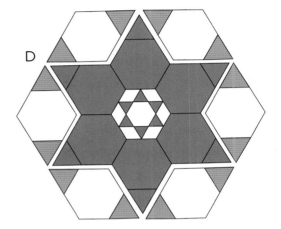

D

7. Sew a large red half-hexagon on each side of the unit from Step 6 to finish the medallion. *Fig. E*

8. Repeat Steps 1–7 to make a total of 12 medallions.

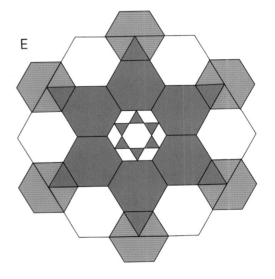

E

SETTING UNITS

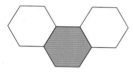

GATHER	20 large red hexagons
	18 large white hexagons
	10 large blue hexagons

1. Sew together 4 red hexagons, 3 white hexagons, and 3 blue hexagons as shown. Repeat to make a second unit.

Make 2.

2. Sew together 2 white hexagons and 1 red hexagon as shown. Repeat to make a second unit.

Make 2.

3. Sew together 2 red hexagons, 3 white hexagons, and 2 blue hexagons as shown. Repeat to make a second unit.

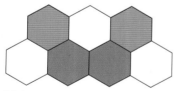

Make 2.

4. Sew together 3 red hexagons and 1 white hexagon as shown. Repeat to make a second unit.

Make 2.

Quilt Assembly

Refer to the quilt layout diagram (next page) while assembling the quilt. Press the horizontal seams up. Swirl the angled intersections around the horizontal seams. (See Pressing Units, page 18.)

Arrange and sew the 12 medallions, 8 setting units, and 2 large red hexagons into the quilt center as shown.

TIP The blocks in this quilt are joined in sections, and the blocks are staggered. It is therefore extremely easy to line up the wrong sides when sewing sections together. To avoid this, arrange the blocks on a large floor or design wall. Place a pin in the hexagon sides you wish to join first, then pick up the blocks and line up the edges with pins, right sides together. As you're sewing the rows, periodically check your work to make sure you haven't accidently sewn incorrect sides together.

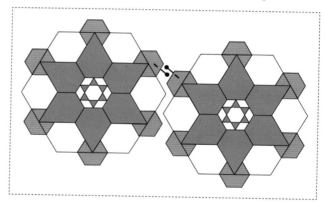

Borders

1. Place the quilt top on a large, flat surface. Slide a rotary cutting mat under the quilt and trim the sides using a long acrylic ruler and rotary cutter. Line up the ¼″ line on the ruler with the marked seam dots at the intersection of the sewn hexagons.

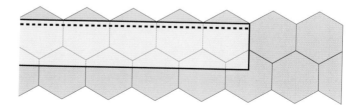

2. Gather the border strips. Refer to Sewing Borders (page 21) to attach the borders to the quilt.

Finishing

1. Cut the backing in thirds to get 3 pieces, each approximately 40″ × 82″. Trim the selvages. Sew together the 3 pieces, right sides together, along a 82″ side. Press the seams.

2. Layer the quilt top with the batting and backing. Baste and quilt as desired. The quilt as shown (page 27) was quilted with an allover curved pattern.

3. Bind the quilt with the binding strips.

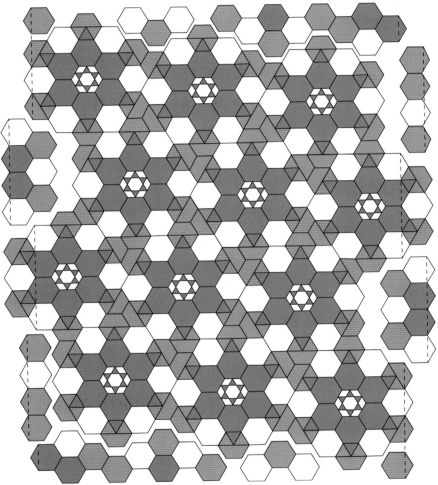

Quilt layout. Dashed lines indicate which patches will be trimmed after all the units are sewn together to square up the quilt.

Meteor Shower

HEXAGON SIZE: 3″ • FINISHED QUILT: 53¼″ × 54½″

MADE BY Emily Breclaw

Fabrics: Laurel Burch for Clothworks

This wallhanging highlights the fun ways you can manipulate hexagons when combining singles and sprockets. The diamonds radiating from the center could never touch point to side like this in a traditional Tumbling Blocks quilt. Use a gradation of colors for the diamonds to create an illusion of depth and movement.

materials

BLUE: 2⅝ yards

TURQUOISE: ⅜ yard

WHITE: ⅜ yard

YELLOW: ¼ yard

ORANGE: ¼ yard

DARK ORANGE: ¼ yard

DARK PINK: ¼ yard

BORDERS: ⅝ yard

BACKING: 3⅓ yards

BINDING: ½ yard

BATTING: 60″ × 61″

cutting

Use the 3″ hexagon family of patterns (pages 105–107). In the instructions that follow, large shapes measure 3″ on a side and small shapes measure 1½″ on a side. Refer to Cutting and Preparing Patches (page 7) as needed.

BLUE

- Cut 8 strips 5¾″ × width of fabric; subcut into 44 large hexagons.
- Cut 8 strips 3⅛″ × width of fabric; subcut into 60 large diamonds and 12 large half-hexagons.
- Cut 2 strips 2″ × width of fabric.
- Cut 6 strips 1¹³⁄₁₆″ × width of fabric; subcut into 36 small half-hexagons, 12 small diamonds, and 54 small triangles.

TURQUOISE

- Cut 2 strips 2″ × width of fabric.
- Cut 3 strips 1¹³⁄₁₆″ × width of fabric; subcut into 36 small diamonds.

WHITE

- Cut 3 strips 3⅛″ × width of fabric; subcut into 25 small hexagons.

YELLOW

- Cut 1 strip 3⅛″ × width of fabric; subcut into 6 large diamonds.

ORANGE

- Cut 1 strip 3⅛″ × width of fabric; subcut into 6 large diamonds.

DARK ORANGE

- Cut 1 strip 3⅛″ × width of fabric; subcut into 6 large diamonds.

DARK PINK

- Cut 1 strip 3⅛″ × width of fabric; subcut into 6 large diamonds.

BORDERS

- Cut 6 strips 3½″ × width of fabric.

BINDING

- Cut 6 strips 2½″ × width of fabric.

construction

Seam allowances are ¼″. Do not sew into the seam allowances. Refer to Sewing Hexagons and Related Shapes (page 15) as needed.

Block Assembly

HALEY SPROCKET

GATHER		
19 small white hexagons	12 small blue diamonds
18 small blue triangles	36 small blue half-hexagons
6 large yellow diamonds	

1. Sew 6 small blue triangles around 1 small white hexagon. *Fig. A*

A

2. Sew 2 small blue triangles to adjacent sides of 1 small white hexagon. Sew a large yellow diamond to this unit, as shown. Repeat to make a total of 6 units. *Fig. B*

3. Sew the 6 units from Step 2 to the unit from Step 1. *Fig. C*

4. Sew 12 small blue half-hexagons to the yellow diamonds. *Fig. D*

5. Sew 6 small white hexagons to the spaces between the diamonds. *Fig. E*

6. Sew 4 small blue half-hexagons and 2 small blue diamonds around 1 small white hexagon as shown. Repeat to make a total of 6 units. *Fig. F*

7. Sew the units from Step 6 to the unit from Step 5 to complete the sprocket. *Fig. G*

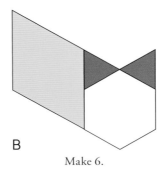

B

Make 6.

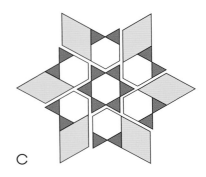

C

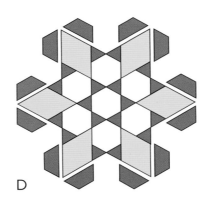

D

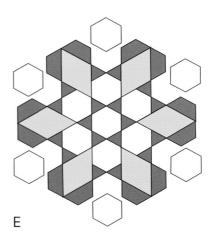

E

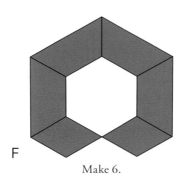

F

Make 6.

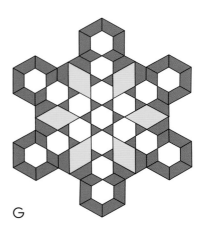

G

COMET TRIPLE

GATHER		
	2 turquoise strips	36 small blue triangles
	2 blue strips	36 small turquoise diamonds
	6 small white hexagons	24 large blue diamonds

1. Sew a turquoise strip to each blue strip, resulting in 2 pieced strips. Using the large diamond template, cut out 12 pieced diamonds that are half blue and half turquoise. (See Cutting Shapes from Pieced Strips, page 9).

2. Sew 6 small blue triangles around 1 small white hexagon. *Fig. H*

3. Sew 6 small turquoise diamonds around the unit from Step 2. *Fig. I*

4. Sew 4 large blue diamonds and 2 pieced diamonds around the unit from Step 3. *Fig. J*

5. Repeat Steps 2–4 to make a total of 6 Comet Triples.

H

I

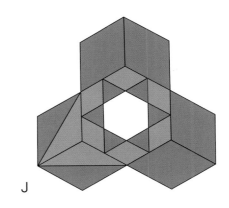

J

TOPSY-TURVY TRIPLE

GATHER		
	6 large blue hexagons	6 large dark orange diamonds
	24 large blue diamonds	6 large dark pink diamonds

1. Sew 2 large blue diamonds to 1 dark orange diamond, as shown. *Fig. K*

2. Sew 2 large blue diamonds to 1 dark pink diamond. *Fig. L*

3. Sew the 2 units from Steps 1 and 2 to a large blue hexagon. *Fig. M*

4. Repeat Steps 1–3 to make a total of 6 Topsy-Turvy Triples.

K

L

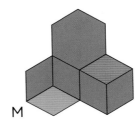

M

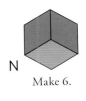

N

Make 6.

TUMBLING SINGLE

GATHER	
	6 large orange diamonds
	12 large blue diamonds

Sew 2 large blue diamonds to a large orange diamond, as shown. Repeat to make a total of 6 Tumbling Singles. *Fig. N*

Quilt Assembly

Refer to the quilt layout diagram (next page) while assembling the rows. Press the vertical seams to the right. Swirl the horizontal seams clockwise around the vertical seams. (See Pressing Units, page 18.)

GATHER	12 large blue half-hexagons
	38 large blue hexagons

1. Sew 8 large blue hexagons into a row. Sew a half-hexagon to each end of the row. Repeat to make a second row. *Fig. O*

2. Sew the Tumbling Singles to the sprocket. Pay careful attention to the direction of the orange diamonds. *Fig. P*

3. Join a Topsy-Turvy Triple to a Comet Triple and a large blue hexagon. Repeat to make a total of 6 units. *Fig. Q*

4. Arrange the units from Step 3 around the center unit from Step 2 and sew them together. *Fig. R*

5. Fill in the remaining spaces with large blue hexagons and half-hexagons, and sew the rows from Step 1 to the top and bottom of the quilt. *Fig. S*

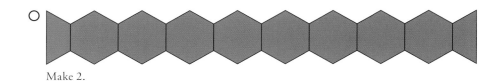

O

Make 2.

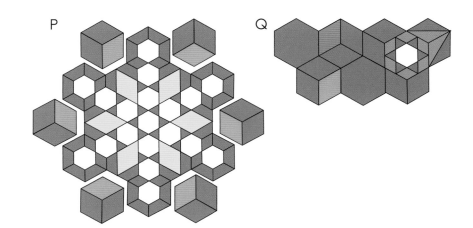

P

Q

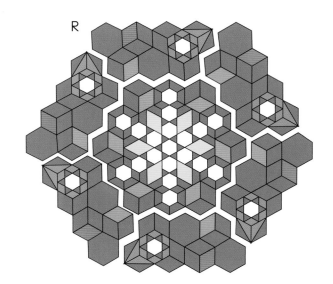

R

S

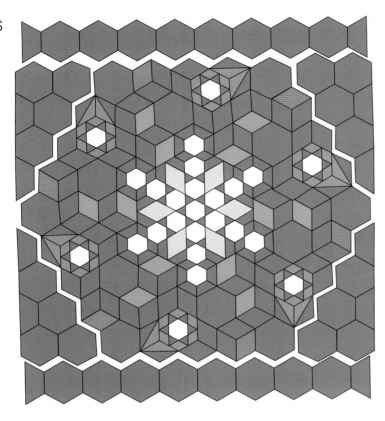

Borders

1. Trim the top and bottom rows of the quilt. See *Independence Day*, Borders, Step 1 (page 30), for how to trim the quilt top.

2. Gather the border strips. Refer to Sewing Borders (page 21) to attach the borders to the quilt.

Finishing

1. Cut the backing in half to get 2 pieces, each approximately 40″ × 60″. Trim the selvages. Sew together the 2 pieces, right sides together, along a 60″ side. Press the seam.

2. Layer the quilt top with the batting and backing. Baste and quilt as desired. The quilt as shown was quilted with curves in the center sprocket, radiating lines curving out gently from the yellow diamond points, and an allover fill of curves in the areas between the radiating lines.

3. Bind the quilt with the binding strips.

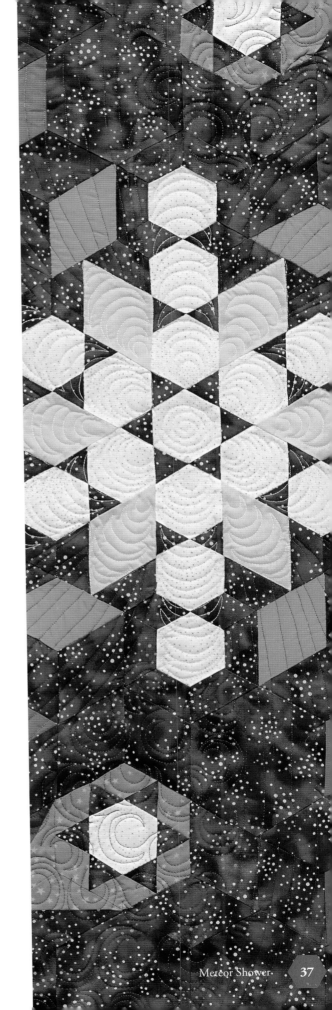

Confetti in Times Square

HEXAGON SIZE: 2″ • FINISHED QUILT: 40″ × 37½″

MADE BY Emily Breclaw

Kite shapes twirl and twinkle around the center of this medallion-style wallhanging. The almost-round border surrounding the sprocket is made up of kite triples and singles. Clever piecing of the triples allows some kites to touch at the sides and others point-to-point, all in the same quilt.

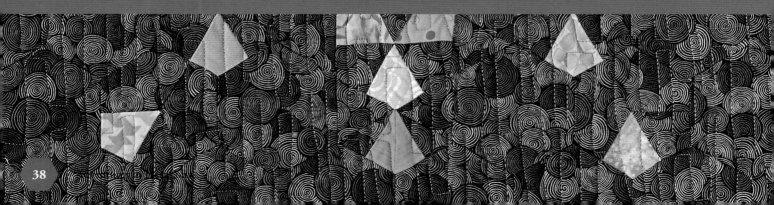

materials

BLACK: 2¼ yards for blocks and borders

GRAY: ¼ yard for blocks

WHITE: ⅛ yard for blocks

ASSORTED BRIGHTS: Scraps to total ⅝ yard; each scrap should measure at least 2½″ × 5″.

BACKING: 2½ yards

BINDING: ½ yard

BATTING: 46″ × 44″

cutting

Use the 2″ hexagon family of patterns (pages 108 and 109). Refer to Cutting and Preparing Patches (page 7) as needed.

BLACK

- Cut 9 strips 4″ × width of fabric; subcut into 68 hexagons.

- Cut 4 strips 3″ × width of fabric for the borders.

- Cut 1 strip 2½″ × width of fabric; subcut 6 house half-hexagons.

- Cut 8 strips 2¼″ × width of fabric; subcut into 10 half-hexagons, 36 kites, 36 triangles, and 6 thirds.

- Cut 3 strips 1¾″ × width of fabric; subcut into 18 rectangles 1¾″ × 5″ for pieced kites.

- Cut 1 strip 1⁹⁄₁₆″ × width of fabric for pieced diamonds.

GRAY

- Cut 2 strips 2¼″ × width of fabric; subcut into 12 diamonds and 6 triangles.

WHITE

- Cut 1 strip 1⁹⁄₁₆″ × width of fabric for pieced diamonds.

ASSORTED BRIGHTS

- Cut 42 kites from scrap fabrics using templates.

- Cut 18 rectangles, 1¾″ × 5″ for pieced kites.

BINDING

- Cut 5 strips 2½″ × width of fabric.

construction

Seam allowances are ¼″. Do not sew into the seam allowances. Refer to Sewing Hexagons and Related Shapes (page 15) as needed.

Block Assembly

SWIRLING SPROCKET

GATHER		
Black and white 1⁹⁄₁₆″ strips	12 gray diamonds
6 black hexagons	6 gray triangles

1. Sew the black strip to the white strip, right sides together, along both sides. Cut 6 diamonds from pieced strip. (Refer to Cutting Shapes from Pieced Strips, page 9).

2. Sew 3 diamonds together, taking note of color placement. Sew a second group of 3 patches in the same way. *Fig. A*

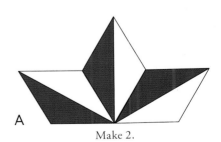

A

Make 2.

3. Sew together the 2 units from Step 2 along the long, flat side. Press, swirling all seams clockwise around the middle intersection. (See Pressing Units, page 18). *Fig. B*

4. Sew a gray triangle to each of the 6 black hexagons. *Fig. C*

5. Sew the units from Step 4 to the unit from Step 3. *Fig. D*

6. Sew the gray diamonds into pairs. Make a total of 6 pairs. *Fig. E*

7. Sew a diamond unit from Step 6 to each black hexagon corner of the star unit. *Figs. F & G*

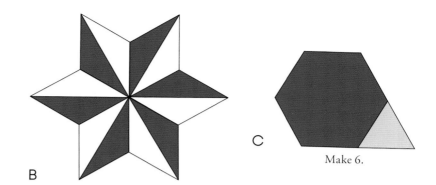

B

C
Make 6.

D

E
Make 6.

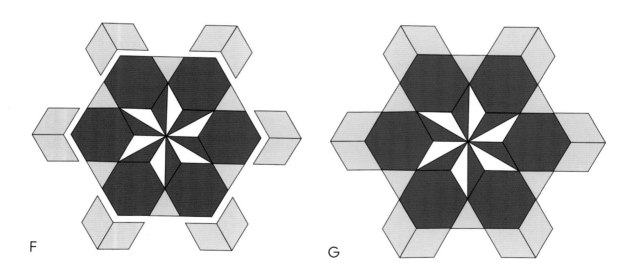

F

G

KITE FESTIVAL TRIPLE

GATHER		
18 bright rectangles	18 black kites
18 black rectangles	36 black triangles
18 bright kites	

1. Sew 1 bright rectangle to each black rectangle. Cut 2 triangles from each rectangle. (Refer to Cutting Shapes from Pieced Strips, page 9.) *Note: Be sure to cut mirror-image triangles by rotating the template 180° after cutting the first triangle. Fig. H*

2. Sew the triangle units into diamonds by sewing the bright sides of the triangles together to form pieced kites. *Fig. I*

3. Sew a black triangle to each of the three diamonds from Step 2. *Fig. J*

4. Sew 3 bright kites and 3 black kites into a hexagon. *Fig. K*

5. Sew a black triangle to each of three sides of the hexagon from Step 4. *Fig. L*

6. Sew the units from Step 3 to the sides of the unit from Step 5. Pay careful attention when sewing to make sure the kites align point to point. *Fig. M*

7. Make 6 Kite Festival Triples. *Fig. N*

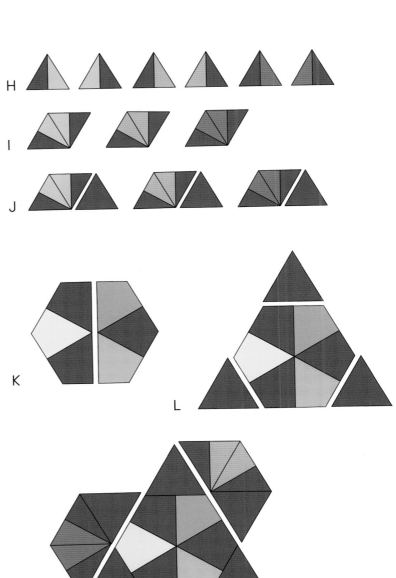

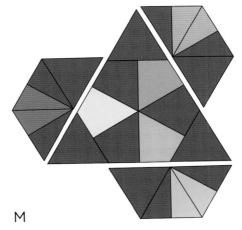

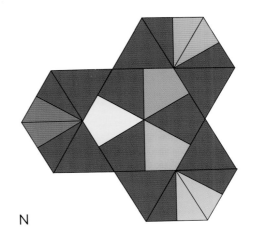

WINDY DAY SINGLE

GATHER	18 bright kites
	18 black kites

1. Arrange 3 black kites and 3 bright kites as shown. *Fig. O*

2. Sew kites into 2 half-hexagons. *Fig. P*

3. Sew the 2 halves together.

4. Make a total of 6 Windy Day Singles. *Fig. Q*

FLYING SOLO SINGLE

GATHER	6 bright kites
	6 black thirds
	6 black house half-hexagons

1. Arrange 1 bright kite, 1 black third, and 1 black house half-hexagon. *Fig. R*

2. Sew the kite to the third. *Fig. S*

3. Sew the 2 halves into a hexagon.

4. Make a total of 6 Flying Solo Singles. *Fig. T*

O

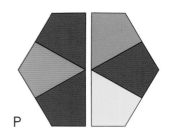

P

Q

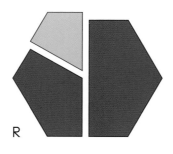

R

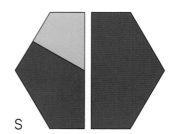

S

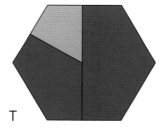

T

Quilt Assembly

Refer to the quilt layout diagram (page 44) while assembling the rows. Press the vertical seams to the right.
Swirl the remaining seams around the vertical seams. (See Pressing Units, page 18.)

1. Sew 10 black hexagons together for row 1. Repeat for row 11.

Make 2.

2. Join the singles, triples, black hexagons, and half-hexagons to create rows 2 and 3 and the identical rows 9 and 10.

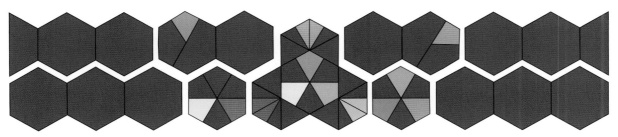

Make 2.

3. Join the singles, triples, black hexagons, and half-hexagons for the center 5 partial rows.
Sew the partial rows to the rosette.

4. Sew together the rows.

Borders

1. Trim the top and bottom rows. See *Independence Day*, Borders, Step 1 (page 30), for how to trim the quilt top.

2. Gather the border strips. Refer to Sewing Borders (page 21) to attach the borders to the quilt.

Finishing

1. Cut the backing in half to get 2 pieces, each approximately 40″ × 45″. Trim the selvages. Sew together the 2 pieces, right sides together, along a 45″ side. Press the seam.

2. Layer the quilt top with the batting and backing. Baste and quilt as desired. The quilt as shown (page 38) was quilted with an allover geometric pattern.

3. Bind the quilt with the binding strips.

Quilt layout

Sparkler

FINISHED HEXAGON BLOCK: 3″ • FINISHED QUILT: 64¾″ × 61½″

PIECED BY Emily Breclaw
QUILTED BY Amy Jameson

Fabrics: Laurel Burch for Clothworks

Color plays a critical role in the radiant effect of this striking quilt. Carefully arranged single blocks emanate from the center rosette.

materials

YELLOW: ½ yard

YELLOW-ORANGE: ⅜ yard

ORANGE: ⅜ yard

DARK ORANGE: ⅜ yard

RED: ½ yard

BLUE: 3¾ yards for blocks and background

BORDER: ⅞ yard

BACKING: 3⅞ yards

BINDING: ⅝ yard

BATTING: 68″ × 71″

cutting

Use the 3″ hexagon family of patterns (pages 105–107). In the instructions that follow, large shapes measure 3″ on a side and small shapes measure 1½″ on a side. Refer to Cutting and Preparing Patches (page 7) as needed.

YELLOW

- Cut 2 strips 3⅛″ × width of fabric; subcut into 13 small hexagons.

- Cut 3 strips 1¹³⁄₁₆″ × width of fabric; subcut into 12 small diamonds and 36 small triangles.

YELLOW-ORANGE

- Cut 1 strip 3⅛″ × width of fabric; subcut into 6 small hexagons.

- Cut 2 strips 1¹³⁄₁₆″ × width of fabric; subcut into 12 small diamonds and 18 small triangles.

ORANGE

- Cut 1 strip 3⅛″ × width of fabric; subcut into 6 small hexagons.

- Cut 3 strips 1¹³⁄₁₆″ × width of fabric; subcut into 18 small diamonds and 18 small triangles.

DARK ORANGE

- Cut 1 strip 3⅛″ × width of fabric; subcut into 6 small hexagons.

- Cut 3 strips 1¹³⁄₁₆″ × width of fabric; subcut into 24 small diamonds and 18 small triangles.

RED

- Cut 8 strips 1¹³⁄₁₆″ × width of fabric; subcut into 138 small diamonds.

BLUE

- Cut 6 strips 5¾″ × width of fabric; subcut into 24 large hexagons and 22 large house half-hexagons.

- Cut 2 strips 3⅛″ × width of fabric; subcut into 12 large half-hexagons.

- Cut 41 strips 1¹³⁄₁₆″ × width of fabric; subcut into 60 small diamonds, 66 small triangles, and 438 small half-hexagons.

BORDERS

- Cut 7 strips 4″ × width of fabric.

BINDING

- Cut 7 strips 2½″ × width of fabric.

---

construction

Seam allowances are ¼″. Do not sew into the seam allowances.
Refer to Sewing Hexagons and Related Shapes (page 15) as needed.

Block Assembly

RADIANT ROSETTE

GATHER		
7 small yellow hexagons	6 small yellow diamonds
18 small blue triangles	18 small yellow triangles
18 small red diamonds	12 small blue diamonds
6 small blue half-hexagons	

1. Sew a small blue triangle to each side of a small yellow hexagon. *Fig. A*

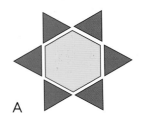

A

2. Sew 6 red diamonds around the sides of the unit from Step 1. *Fig. B*

3. Sew 6 blue half-hexagons around the unit from Step 2. *Fig. C*

4. Sew together 1 yellow and 2 red small diamonds to make a hexagon. Repeat to make a total of 6 hexagons. *Fig. D*

5. Sew the hexagons from Step 4 to the unit from Step 3, making sure that the yellow diamond in each hexagon points outward. Only the red diamonds will be sewn into the unit at this time. *Fig. E*

6. Sew 3 small yellow triangles to adjacent sides of a small yellow hexagon. *Fig. F*

7. Sew a small blue diamond between each of the triangles. Sew small blue triangles to the remaining triangle sides. Repeat to make a total of 6 units. *Fig. G*

8. Sew the units from Step 7 to the unit from Step 5 to complete the rosette. *Fig. H*

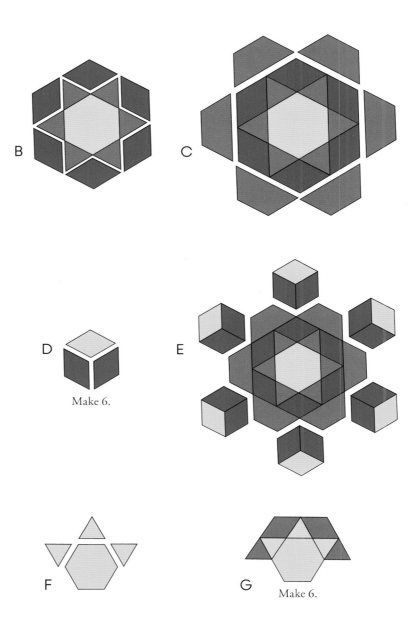

B

C

D

Make 6.

E

F

G   Make 6.

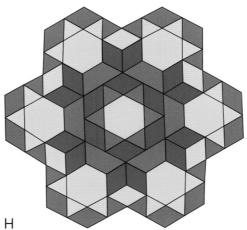

H

SMALL SUN SINGLE

GATHER	6 small yellow hexagons	18 small yellow-orange triangles	6 small dark orange hexagons	48 small blue diamonds
	18 small yellow triangles	6 small orange hexagons	18 small dark orange triangles	48 small blue triangles
	6 small yellow-orange hexagons	18 small orange triangles	72 small blue half-hexagons	

1. Sew 3 small yellow triangles to adjacent sides of a small yellow hexagon.

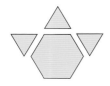

2. Sew a blue diamond between the yellow triangles and a blue triangle to the remaining yellow triangle sides.

3. Sew a blue half-hexagon to each remaining side of the yellow hexagon.

4. Repeat to make a total of 6 singles.

Make 6.

5. Repeat Steps 1–3 with yellow-orange hexagons and triangles. Make a total of 6 singles.

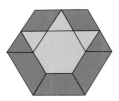

Make 6.

6. Repeat Steps 1–3 with orange hexagons and triangles. Make a total of 6 singles.

Make 6.

7. Repeat Steps 1–3 with dark orange hexagons and triangles. Make a total of 6 singles.

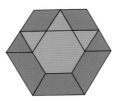

Make 6.

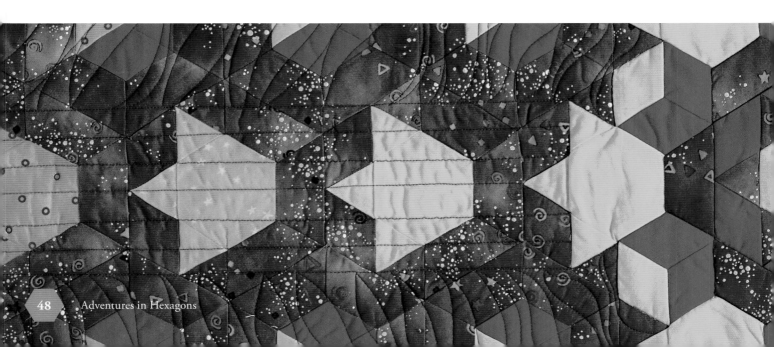

FRAMED BLOCK SINGLE

GATHER	
6 small yellow diamonds	24 small dark orange diamonds
12 small yellow-orange diamonds	120 small red diamonds
18 small orange diamonds	360 small blue half-hexagons

1. Sew together 2 small red diamonds and 1 small yellow diamond to form a hexagon.

2. Sew a blue half-hexagon to each side of the unit from Step 1.

3. Repeat to make a total of 6 blocks with yellow diamonds.

Make 6.

4. Repeat Steps 1 and 2 with the yellow-orange diamonds. Make a total of 12 blocks.

Make 12.

5. Repeat Steps 1 and 2 with the orange diamonds. Make a total of 18 blocks.

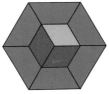

Make 18.

6. Repeat Steps 1 and 2 with the dark orange diamonds. Make a total of 24 blocks.

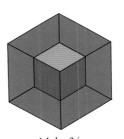

Make 24.

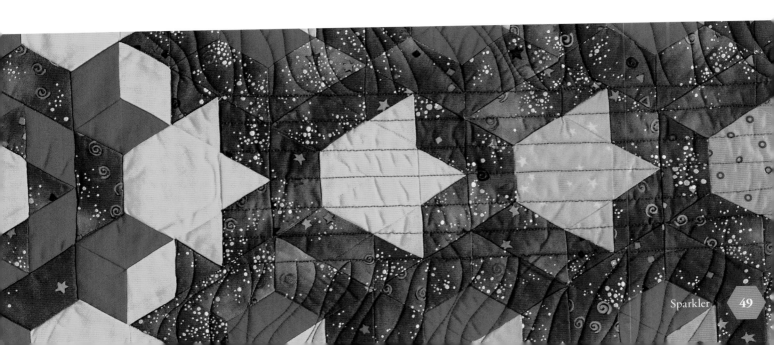

Quilt Assembly

Refer to the quilt layout diagram (page 52) while assembling the rows. Press the vertical seams to the right. Swirl the horizontal seams clockwise around the vertical seams. (See Pressing Units, page 18.)

1. Sew together 4 Small Sun Singles.

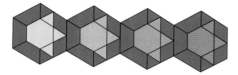

2. Sew together 4 Framed Block Singles and 1 blue half-hexagon. Pay careful attention to the diamond arrangement to maintain the radiant effect.

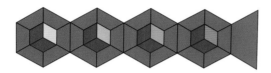

3. Sew together a second partial row of 4 Framed Block Singles and 1 blue half-hexagon. Note that this row differs from Step 2 in the arrangement of the non-red diamonds.

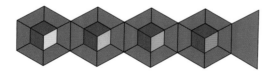

4. Join the row from Step 2 to the row from Step 1.

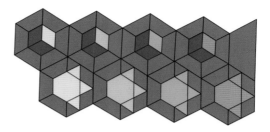

5. Join the row from Step 3 to the unit from Step 4.

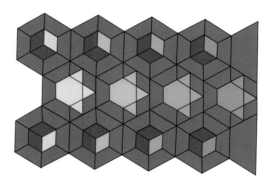

6. Repeat Steps 1–5 to make an identical partial row.

7. Sew the partial rows to either side of the Radiant Rosette.

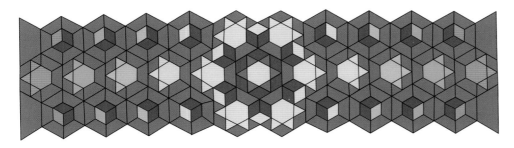

8. Make 2 each of the next 4 rows. One will be sewn above the rosette rows, and one will be rotated 180° and sewn below the center rows. Pay careful attention to the arrangement of the blocks to maintain the radiant effect.

Make 2 rows.

Make 2 rows.

Make 2 rows.

Make 2 rows.

9. Take the 22 house half-hexagons and sew them into 2 rows of 11 house half-hexagons each.

10. Sew together the rows, following the quilt layout diagram.

Borders

Gather the border strips. Refer to Sewing Borders (page 21) to attach the borders to the quilt.

Finishing

1. Cut the backing in half to get 2 pieces, each approximately 40″ × 69″. Trim the selvages. Sew together the 2 pieces, right sides together, along a 69″ side. Press the seam.

2. Layer the quilt top with the batting and backing. Baste and quilt as desired. The quilt as shown (page 45) was custom quilted. The center rosette was stitched in-the-ditch, straight lines were quilted through the Small Sun Singles, wavy lines connect the Framed Block Singles, and the outer edges of the quilt were stitched with a meandering pattern.

3. Bind the quilt with the binding strips.

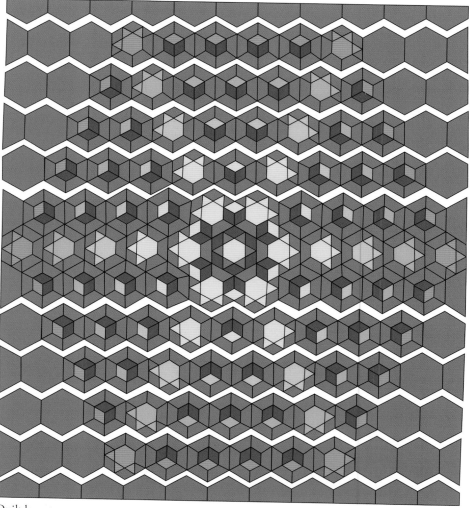

Quilt layout

Starburst

HEXAGON SIZE: 3″ • FINISHED QUILT: 58½″ × 78½″

PIECED BY Emily Breclaw
QUILTED BY Amy Jameson

Changing the colors of one rosette and the surrounding singles creates an interesting off-center focal point for this cheerful quilt. Create a completely different look by substituting a different choice of singles and rosettes. See Design Primer (page 100) for an example with different rosettes and singles.

materials

ORANGE: 3⅝ yards

PINK: ⅞ yard

YELLOW: ½ yard

LAVENDER: ⅜ yard

DARK PINK: ⅜ yard

PURPLE: ¼ yard

DARK YELLOW: ⅛ yard

ACCENT DARK PINK: ¼ yard

DARK PURPLE: ¼ yard

BORDER: ⅞ yard

BACKING: 4¾ yards

BINDING: ⅝ yard

BATTING: 65″ × 85″

cutting

Use the 3″ hexagon family of patterns (pages 105–107). In the instructions that follow, large shapes measure 3″ on a side and small shapes measure 1½″ on a side. Refer to Cutting and Preparing Patches (page 7) as needed.

ORANGE

- Cut 5 strips 5¾″ × width of fabric; subcut into 28 large hexagons.

- Cut 4 strips 3½″ × width of fabric; subcut into 22 large house half-hexagons.

- Cut 10 strips 3⅛″ × width of fabric; subcut into 78 small hexagons and 14 large half-hexagons.

- Cut 26 strips 1¹³⁄₁₆″ × width of fabric; subcut into 234 small half-hexagons and 144 small diamonds.

PINK

- Cut 7 strips 3⅛″ × width of fabric; subcut into 72 small hexagons.

- Cut 3 strips 1¹³⁄₁₆″ × width of fabric; subcut into 72 small triangles.

YELLOW

- Cut 9 strips 1¹³⁄₁₆″ × width of fabric; subcut into 144 small diamonds.

LAVENDER

- Cut 7 strips 1¹³⁄₁₆″ × width of fabric; subcut into 180 small triangles.

DARK PINK

- Cut 3 strips 3⅛″ × width of fabric; subcut into 30 small hexagons.

PURPLE

- Cut 2 strips 1¹³⁄₁₆″ × width of fabric; subcut into 42 small triangles.

DARK YELLOW

- Cut 1 strip 1¹³⁄₁₆″ × width of fabric; subcut into 12 small diamonds.

ACCENT DARK PINK

- Cut 1 strip 3⅛″ × width of fabric; subcut into 6 small hexagons.

- Cut 1 strip 1¹³⁄₁₆″ × width of fabric; subcut into 6 small triangles.

DARK PURPLE

- Cut 1 strip 3⅛″ × width of fabric; subcut into 7 small hexagons.

BORDERS

- Cut 7 strips 3½″ × width of fabric.

BINDING

- Cut 8 strips 2½″ × width of fabric.

construction

Seam allowances are ¼″. Do not sew into the seam allowances.
Refer to Sewing Hexagons and Related Shapes (page 15) as needed.

Block Assembly

SUNSHINE ROSETTE

GATHER		
12 small dark pink hexagons	72 small orange hexagons
72 small lavender triangles	216 small orange half-hexagons
144 small yellow diamonds	72 small pink hexagons
72 small pink triangles	

1. Sew 1 small lavender triangle and 1 small pink triangle to adjacent sides of a small yellow diamond. *Fig. A*

2. Sew a second yellow diamond to the other sides of the triangles. *Fig. B*

3. Repeat to make a total of 6 pieced hexagons. *Fig. C*

4. Sew the pieced hexagons from Step 3 around a dark pink hexagon. Make sure the purple triangles touch the center hexagon. *Fig. D*

5. Sew 6 small orange hexagons around the unit from Step 4. *Fig. E*

6. Sew the short sides of 3 small orange half-hexagons to adjacent sides of a small pink hexagon. *Fig. F*

7. Repeat Step 6 to make a total of 6 units. *Fig. G*

8. Sew the units from Step 7 around the unit from Step 5. If you are hand sewing, these can be sewn consecutively without breaking the thread between units. *Fig. H*

9. Repeat Steps 1–8 to make a total of 12 rosettes. *Fig. I*

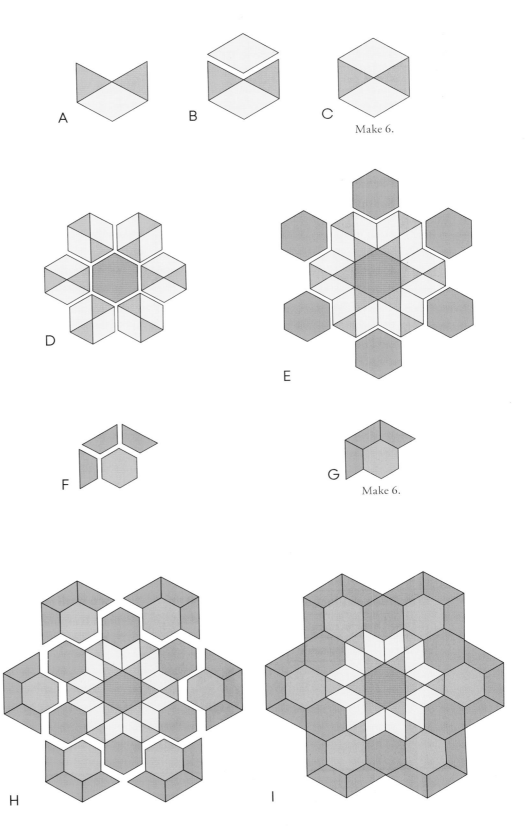

A   B   C
Make 6.

D

E

F   G
Make 6.

H   I

ACCENT SUNSHINE ROSETTE

GATHER			
	1 small dark purple hexagon		6 small accent dark pink hexagons
	6 small purple triangles		6 small orange hexagons
	12 small dark yellow diamonds		18 small orange half-hexagons
	6 small accent dark pink triangles		

The Accent Sunshine Rosette is made in much the same way as the Sunshine Rosette (page 54), using the darker colored fabrics as noted in the steps that follow.

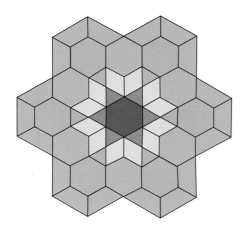

1. Sew 1 small purple triangle and 1 small accent dark pink triangle to adjacent sides of the small dark yellow diamond, as shown.

2. Sew a second dark yellow diamond to the other sides of the triangles.

3. Repeat to make a total of 6 pieced hexagons.

4. Sew the pieced hexagons from Step 3 around a small dark purple hexagon. Make sure the purple triangles touch the center hexagon.

5. Sew 6 small orange hexagons around the unit from Step 4.

6. Sew the short sides of 3 small orange half-hexagons to adjacent sides of a small dark pink hexagon.

7. Repeat Step 6 to make a total of 6 units.

8. Sew the units from Step 7 around the unit from Step 5. If you are hand sewing, these can be sewn consecutively without breaking the thread between units.

STARRY SINGLE

GATHER	
	18 small dark pink hexagons
	108 small lavender triangles
	108 small orange diamonds

1. Sew 6 small lavender triangles around small dark pink hexagon.

2. Sew 6 small orange diamonds around the unit from Step 1.

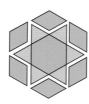

3. Repeat to make a total of 18 Starry Singles.

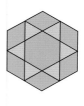

ACCENT STARRY SINGLE

GATHER	
	6 small dark purple hexagons
	36 small purple triangles
	36 small orange diamonds

1. Follow Starry Single, Steps 1–3 (above), replacing the small dark pink hexagon with a small dark purple hexagon and the small lavender triangles with small purple triangles.

2. Repeat to make a total of 6 Accent Starry Singles.

Quilt Assembly

Refer to the quilt layout diagram (page 59) while assembling the rows. Press the vertical seams to the right. Swirl the horizontal seams clockwise around the vertical seams. (See Pressing Units, page 18.)

GATHER	28 large orange hexagons
	14 large orange half-hexagons
	22 large orange house half-hexagons

1. Sew 11 large house half-hexagons in a row along the short sides. Repeat to make a second row.

Make 2.

2. Join the singles, rosettes, orange hexagons, and orange half-hexagons as shown to make the first row.

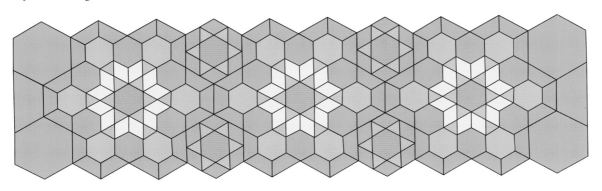

3. Join the singles, rosettes, orange hexagons, and orange half-hexagons as shown to make the second row.

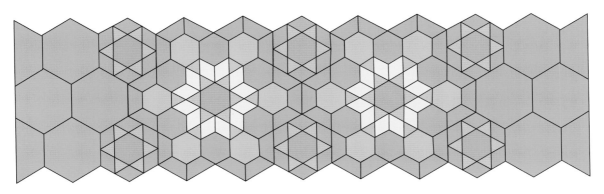

4. Join the singles, accent single, rosettes, orange hexagons, and orange half-hexagons to make the third row.

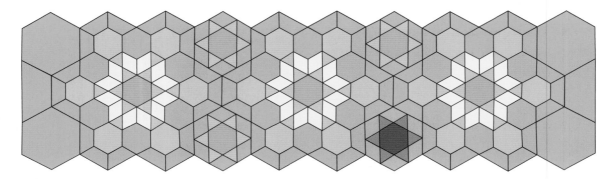

5. Join the singles, accent singles, accent rosette, rosette, orange hexagons, and orange half-hexagons to make the fourth row.

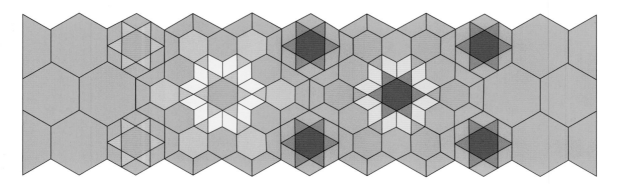

6. Join the rosettes, singles, accent single, orange hexagons, and orange half-hexagons to make the fifth row.

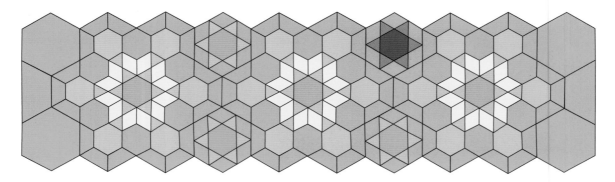

7. Sew together the rows.

8. Sew the rows of house half-hexagons to the top and bottom of the quilt.

9. Trim the sections of the house half-hexagons that extend beyond the sides of the quilt top flush with the top.

Borders

Gather the border strips. Refer to Sewing Borders (page 21) to attach the borders to the quilt.

Finishing

1. Cut the backing in half to get 2 pieces, each approximately 40″ × 85″. Trim the selvages. Sew together the 2 pieces, right sides together, along an 85″ side. Press the seam.

2. Layer the quilt top with the batting and backing. Baste and quilt as desired. The quilt as shown (page 53) was quilted with an allover loopy pattern, with some custom spirals and designs in the accent rosette.

3. Bind the quilt with the binding strips.

Quilt layout

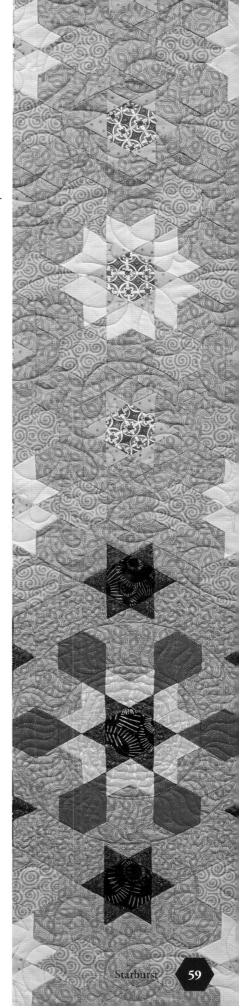

Twinkling

HEXAGON SIZE: 3″ • FINISHED QUILT: 58½″ × 69½″

PIECED BY Emily Breclaw
QUILTED BY Amy Jameson

Kites in the background blocks accent the prismatic effect of the bejeweled sprockets scattered on this lap-size quilt.

materials

DARK BLUE: ¼ yard

DARK PINK: ¼ yard

DARK YELLOW: ¼ yard

DARK GREEN: ¼ yard

DARK PURPLE: ¼ yard

LIGHT BLUE: ¼ yard

LIGHT PINK: ¼ yard

LIGHT YELLOW: ¼ yard

LIGHT GREEN: ¼ yard

LIGHT PURPLE: ¼ yard

LIGHT GRAY: 1⅝ yards

ASSORTED GRAYS: To total
1¾ yards

BORDERS: ⅞ yard

BACKING: 3¾ yards

BINDING: ⅝ yard

BATTING: 65″ × 76″

cutting

Use the 3″ hexagon family of patterns (pages 105–107). Refer to Cutting and Preparing Patches (page 7) as needed.

DARK BLUE

- Cut 1 strip 3⅛″ × width of fabric; subcut into 6 thirds.
- Cut 1 strip 2¹³⁄₁₆″ × width of fabric; subcut into 15 kites.

DARK PINK

- Cut 1 strip 3⅛″ × width of fabric; subcut into 6 thirds.
- Cut 1 strip 2¹³⁄₁₆″ × width of fabric; subcut into 15 kites.

DARK YELLOW

- Cut 1 strip 3⅛″ × width of fabric; subcut into 6 thirds.
- Cut 1 strip 2¹³⁄₁₆″ × width of fabric; subcut into 15 kites.

DARK PURPLE

- Cut 1 strip 3⅛″ × width of fabric; subcut into 6 thirds.
- Cut 1 strip 2¹³⁄₁₆″ × width of fabric; subcut into 15 kites.

DARK GREEN

- Cut 1 strip 3⅛″ × width of fabric; subcut into 6 thirds.
- Cut 1 strip 2¹³⁄₁₆″ × width of fabric; subcut into 15 kites.

LIGHT BLUE

- Cut 1 strip 3⅛″ × width of fabric; subcut into 6 thirds.
- Cut 1 strip 2¹³⁄₁₆″ × width of fabric; subcut into 16 kites.

LIGHT PINK

- Cut 1 strip 3⅛″ × width of fabric; subcut into 6 thirds.
- Cut 1 strip 2¹³⁄₁₆″ × width of fabric; subcut into 16 kites.

LIGHT YELLOW

- Cut 1 strip 3⅛″ × width of fabric; subcut into 6 thirds.
- Cut 1 strip 2¹³⁄₁₆″ × width of fabric; subcut into 16 kites.

LIGHT GREEN

- Cut 1 strip 3⅛″ × width of fabric; subcut into 6 thirds.
- Cut 1 strip 2¹³⁄₁₆″ × width of fabric; subcut into 16 kites.

LIGHT PURPLE

- Cut 1 strip 3⅛″ × width of fabric; subcut into 6 thirds.
- Cut 1 strip 2¹³⁄₁₆″ × width of fabric; subcut into 16 kites.

LIGHT GRAY

- Cut 2 strips 5¾″ × width of fabric; subcut into 11 hexagons.
- Cut 11 strips 3⅛″ × width of fabric; subcut into 15 half-hexagons and 60 thirds.
- Cut 1 strip 3½″ × width of fabric; subcut into 6 house half-hexagons.

ASSORTED GRAYS

- Cut 21 strips 2¹³⁄₁₆″ × width of fabric; subcut into 328 kites.

BORDERS

- Cut 7 strips 3½″ × width of fabric.

BINDING

- Cut 7 strips 2½″ × width of fabric.

construction

Seam allowances are ¼". Do not sew into the seam allowances.
Refer to Sewing Hexagons and Related Shapes (page 15) as needed.

Block Assembly

BRILLIANT SPROCKET

1. Sew 3 dark blue kites and 3 light blue kites into 2 half-hexagons, alternating colors. Press to the right. *Fig. A*

2. Sew the halves together. Press half of the seam up and half down so all seams swirl counter-clockwise around the center. (See Pressing Units, page 18.) *Fig. B*

3. Sew together 1 dark blue third, 1 light blue third, 1 dark blue kite, and 1 light blue kite. Be careful not to sew the mirror image of the block. Press the seams open. *Fig. C*

4. Repeat Step 3 to make a total of 6 hexagons.

5. Sew together 2 light gray thirds, 1 dark blue kite, and 1 gray kite. *Fig. D*

6. Repeat Step 5 to make a total of 6 hexagons.

7. Arrange the blocks and sew them into rows. *Fig. E*

8. Sew together the rows to complete the sprocket. *Fig. F*

GATHER	All dark kites and thirds	All light gray thirds
	All light thirds	30 assorted gray kites
	9 of each color of the light-colored kites	

A

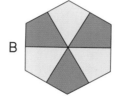

B

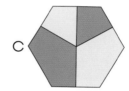

C

D

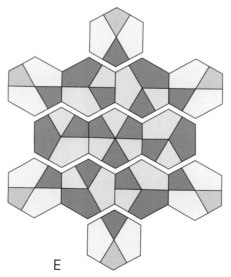

E

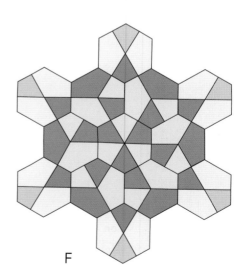

F

9. Repeat Steps 1–8 with the dark and light pink shapes.

10. Repeat Steps 1–8 with the dark and light green shapes.

11. Repeat Steps 1–8 with the dark and light yellow shapes.

12. Repeat Steps 1–8 with the dark and light purple shapes.

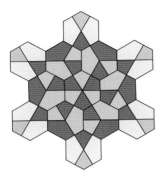 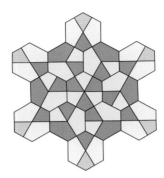 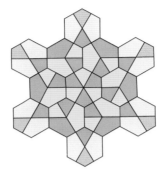 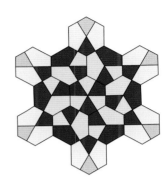

PRISMATIC SINGLE

GATHER Remaining gray and light kites

1. Sew 6 kites from different fabrics, 2 groups of 3. Press the seams to the right.

2. Sew together the 2 groups along the long flat side. Press half of the seam up and the other half down so that all the seams swirl counter-clockwise. (See Pressing Units, page 18.)

3. Repeat Steps 1 and 2 to make a total of 50 Prismatic Singles.

4. With the remaining kites, make 11 half-blocks.

Make 11.

Quilt Assembly

Refer to the quilt layout diagram (page 64) while assembling. Press the vertical seams to the right. Swirl the remaining seams around the vertical seams. (See Pressing Units, page 18.)

1. Arrange the blocks on a design wall or large floor space. Sew the singles and sprockets into clusters. Then join the clusters into the quilt top.

2. Trim the blocks indicated by the dashed lines to square up the quilt top.

Borders

Gather the border strips. Refer to Sewing Borders (page 21) to attach the borders to the quilt.

Finishing

1. Cut the backing in half to get 2 pieces, each approximately 40″ × 67″. Trim the selvages. Sew together the 2 pieces, right sides together, along a 67″ side. Press the seam.

2. Layer the quilt top with the batting and backing. Baste and quilt as desired. The quilt as shown (page 60) was quilted with a meandering boxes pattern.

3. Bind the quilt with the binding strips.

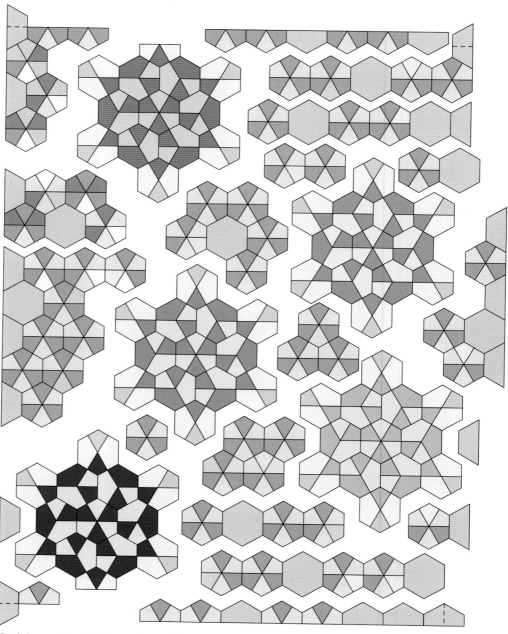

Quilt layout. Dashed lines indicate which patches will be trimmed after all the units are sewn together to square up the quilt.

Hello, Orion

HEXAGON SIZE: 3" • FINISHED QUILT: 59½" × 70½"

MADE BY Emily Breclaw

Fabrics: Japanese indigo, taupe, and dobby weave fabrics

A variety of single stars and hexagons gives this quilt the illusion of a constellation. The off-center hexagons are created with a unique Log Cabin technique that creates lots of scraps. Save them for the stars in *Stardust and Moonbeams* (page 73).

materials

WHITE: ⅝ yard

YELLOW: ⅛ yard

ORANGE: ½ yard

INDIGO: 8 yards

BORDER: ¾ yard

BACKING: 3¾ yards

BINDING: ⅝ yard

BATTING: 66″ × 77″

cutting

Use the 3″ hexagon family of patterns (pages 105–107). In the instructions that follow, large shapes measure 3″ on a side, small shapes measure 1½″ on a side, and very small shapes measure ¾″ on a side. Refer to Cutting and Preparing Patches (page 7) as needed.

WHITE

- Cut 2 strips 3⅛″ × width of fabric; subcut into 14 small hexagons.

- Cut 5 strips 1¹³⁄₁₆″ × width of fabric; subcut into 16 very small hexagons and 96 small triangles.

YELLOW

- Cut 1 strip 1¹³⁄₁₆″ × width of fabric; subcut into 16 very small hexagons.

ORANGE

- Cut 3 strips 3⅛″ × width of fabric; subcut into 24 small hexagons.

- Cut 1 strip 1¹³⁄₁₆″ × width of fabric; subcut into 14 very small hexagons.

INDIGO

- Cut 8 strips 5¾″ × width of fabric; subcut into 48 large hexagons.

TIP To conserve fabric, save the leftover triangles you cut between the hexagons on the 5¾″ strips. Use these triangles instead of the 3″ × 2″ rectangles and the 4″ × 1½″ rectangles listed in Skewed Single, Step 1 (next page), and Wonky Single, Step 1 (page 69).

- Cut 36–37 strips 4″ × width of fabric, 36 if using the scraps as indicated in the Tip (above).

- Cut 5 strips 3½″ × width of fabric; subcut into 26 large house half-hexagons.

- Cut 2 strips 3⅛″ × width of fabric; subcut into 11 large half-hexagons.

- Cut 17–19 strips 3″ × width of fabric, 17 if using the scraps as indicated in the Tip (above).

- Cut 6 strips 1¹³⁄₁₆″ × width of fabric; subcut into 96 small diamonds.

BORDERS

- Cut 7 strips 3″ × width of fabric.

BINDING

- Cut 8 strips 2½″ × width of fabric.

construction

Seam allowances are ¼″. Do not sew into the seam allowances unless otherwise indicated. Refer to Sewing Hexagons and Related Shapes (page 15) as needed. Note: When template pieced, the Wonky and Skewed Singles will yield many scraps of unusual sizes. Save them to use in Stardust and Moonbeams (page 73).

Block Assembly

STARRY SINGLE

GATHER	16 small orange hexagons
	96 small white triangles
	96 small indigo diamonds

1. Sew 6 small white triangles around a small orange hexagon.

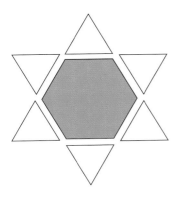

2. Sew 6 small indigo diamonds around unit from Step 1.

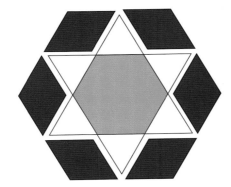

3. Repeat to make a total of 16 Starry Singles.

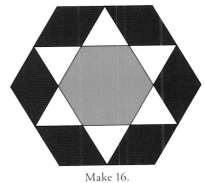

Make 16.

SKEWED SINGLE

IMPORTANT: Seams sewn within these singles are stitched edge to edge instead of dot to dot.

GATHER	14 small white hexagons
	8 small orange hexagons
	3″ indigo strips

TIP | SKEWED SINGLE ENGLISH PAPER PIECING

These blocks and the Wonky Singles (page 69) are sewn Log-Cabin style, with a strip of indigo sewn to each side of the hexagon and trimmed before adding the next strip. At the end, you will have a strange-looking patch with the hexagon roughly in the center and uneven edges. These will all be trimmed away, creating highly unusual hexagons. If you are using English paper piecing for this quilt, use the Skewed Singles Log Cabin pattern (page 110). Cut this pattern apart into the 7 pieces and cut pieces 2–7 from the 3″ indigo strips. Piece them in numerical order.

1. Place a scrap left over from cutting the indigo hexagons *or* a 2″ × 3″ rectangle cut from an indigo strip right sides together with a small white hexagon. Place the rectangle with about ¼″ of the rectangle overhanging the side of the hexagon. Sew together and then press toward the indigo. *Fig. A*

2. Trim the edge of the indigo rectangle flush with the next side of the hexagon. *Fig. B*

3. Cut a rectangle of indigo roughly 3″ × 4½″ and sew it to the second side of the hexagon (including the first indigo strip). Press toward the indigo. *Fig. C*

4. Trim the edge of the second indigo rectangle flush with the third side of the hexagon. *Fig. D*

TIP | If you have an acrylic ruler with 60° lines, it can be very helpful when trimming these sides. Align the straight edge of the ruler with the side of the hexagon to sew next, and line the 60° line with the next side of the hexagon.

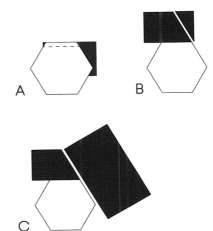

5. Cut a rectangle of indigo roughly 3″ × 5″. Sew it to the third side of the hexagon (including the second indigo strip). Press toward the indigo. *Fig. E*

6. Trim the edge of the third indigo rectangle flush with the fourth side of the hexagon. *Fig. F*

7. In the same manner, sew 3″ × 5″ rectangles to the fourth and fifth sides of the hexagon. Press toward the indigo. *Figs. G–I*

8. Trim the edges of the first and fifth rectangles flush with the final side of the hexagon. Cut a rectangle of indigo roughly 3″ × 8½″ and sew it to the last side of the hexagon. Press toward the indigo. *Figs. J & K*

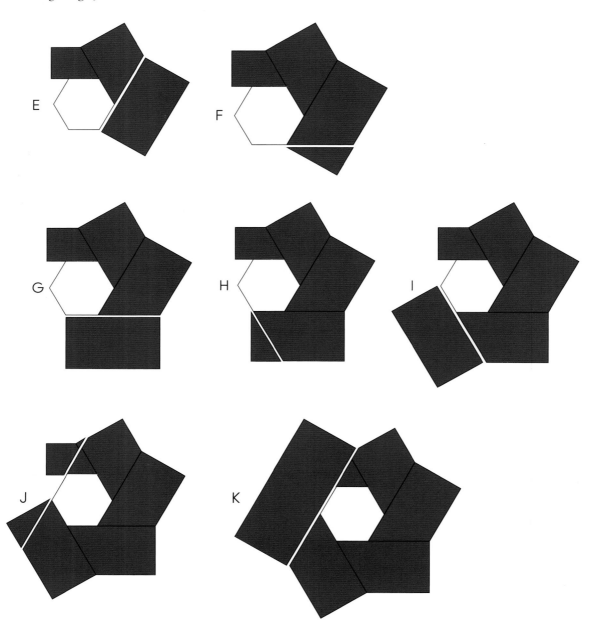

9. Place a 3″ clear hexagon template on top of the block. Turn the hexagon until you are satisfied with the look of the block. (I tried to avoid cutting away any of the little animal or people motifs on the fabric I was using.) Also, to make it easier to sew the hexagons together, check to make sure none of the seam allowances cross the 3″ hexagon corners exactly. Cut a 3″ hexagon out of your pieced block. *Note: This is a good time to use a rotating cutting mat if you have one. Fig. L*

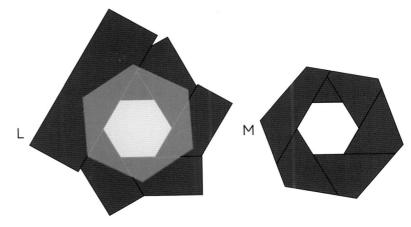

10. Repeat Steps 1–9 to make a total of 22 Skewed Singles, of which 14 will have a white center hexagon and 8 will have an orange center hexagon. *Fig. M*

WONKY SINGLE

IMPORTANT: *Seams sewn within these singles are stitched edge to edge instead of dot to dot.*

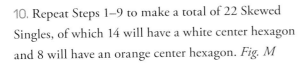

GATHER		
	16 very small yellow hexagons	16 very small white hexagons
	14 very small orange hexagons	4″ indigo strips

This block is pieced in essentially the same manner as the Skewed Single. The only difference is a smaller central hexagon and wider indigo rectangles.

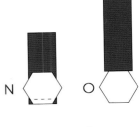

TIP WONKY SINGLE ENGLISH PAPER PIECING

If you are using English paper piecing for this quilt, use the Wonky Single Log Cabin pattern (page 110) to make the Wonky Single. Follow the directions as given for Tip: Skewed Single English Paper Piecing (page 67).

1. Place a scrap left over from cutting the indigo hexagons *or* a 1½″ × 4″ rectangle cut from an indigo strip right sides together with a very small yellow hexagon. Place the rectangle with about ¼″ of the rectangle overhanging the side of the hexagon. Sew together and then press toward the indigo. *Fig. N*

2. Trim the edge of the indigo rectangle flush with the next side of the hexagon. *Fig. O*

3. Cut a square of indigo roughly 4″ × 4″. Sew it to the second side of the hexagon (including the first indigo strip). Press toward the indigo. *Fig. P*

4. Trim the edge of the second indigo rectangle flush with the third side of the hexagon. *Fig. Q*

TIP If you have an acrylic ruler with 60° lines, use it as you did for the Skewed Single (page 67).

5. Cut a rectangle of indigo roughly 4″ × 5″. Sew it to the third side of the hexagon (including the second indigo strip). Press toward the indigo. *Fig. R*

6. Trim the edge of the third indigo rectangle flush with the fourth side of the hexagon. *Fig. S*

7. In the same manner, sew 4″ × 5″ rectangles to the fourth and fifth sides of the hexagon. Press toward the indigo. *Figs. T–V*

8. Trim the edges of the first and fifth rectangles flush with the final side of the hexagon. Cut a rectangle of indigo roughly 3″ × 8½″ and sew to the last side of the hexagon. Press toward the indigo. *Figs. W & X*

9. Place a 3″ clear hexagon template on top of the block. Turn the hexagon until you are satisfied with the look of the block. (I tried to avoid cutting away any of the little animal or people motifs on the fabric I was using).

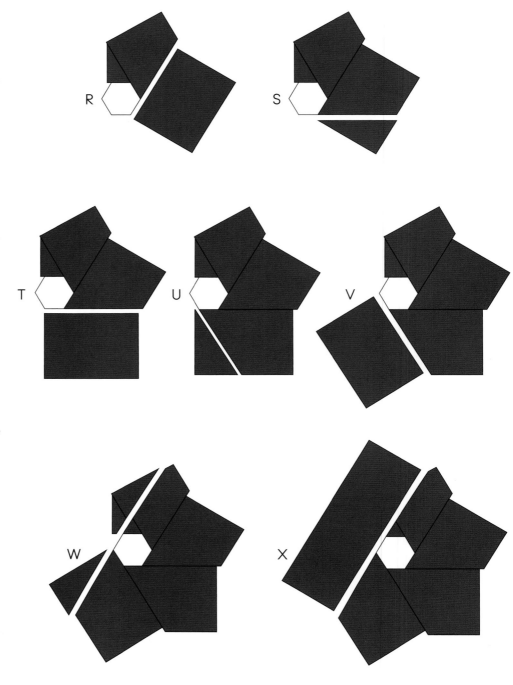

Also, to make it easier to sew the hexagons together, check to make sure none of the seam allowances cross the 3″ hexagon corners exactly. Cut a 3″ hexagon out of your pieced block. *Note: This is a good time to use a rotating cutting mat if you have one.* Fig. Y

10. Repeat Steps 1–9 to make a total of 46 Skewed Singles, of which 16 will have white centers, 16 will have yellow centers, and 14 will have orange centers. *Fig. Z*

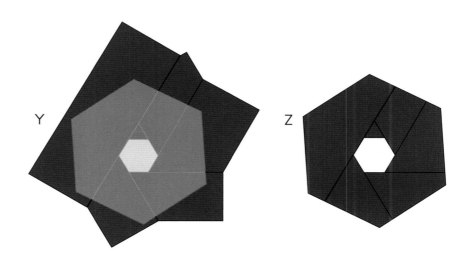

Quilt Assembly

Refer to the quilt layout diagram (page 72) while assembling the columns. Press the horizontal seams up (toward the top of the quilt). Swirl the remaining seams around the horizontal seams. (See Pressing Units, page 18.)

GATHER		
Starry, Skewed, and Wonky Singles	Large indigo half-hexagons	
Large indigo hexagons	Large house half-hexagons	

TIP With all the unusual seams in the Skewed and Wonky Singles, it can be confusing to align the hexagons when sewing them into columns. Change your sewing machine thread to a slightly different color when you begin sewing blocks together to make it easier to see which seams need to be aligned.

1. On a design wall or large floor space, arrange the hexagons and half-hexagons

Sew the hexagons together in columns. Press the seams up, toward the quilt top.

2. Sew the columns of hexagons together.

3. Sew the house half-hexagons into 2 columns of 13, sewing along a short side.

4. Sew one column of house half-hexagons to the left side of the quilt and one to the right. Trim the excess house half-hexagons flush with the quilt top and bottom.

Borders

Gather the border strips. Refer to Sewing Borders (page 21) to attach the borders to the quilt.

Finishing

1. Cut the backing in half to get 2 pieces, each approximately 40″ × 67″. Trim the selvages. Sew together the 2 pieces, right sides together, along a 67″ side. Press the seam.

2. Layer the quilt top with the batting and backing. Baste and quilt as desired. The quilt as shown (page 65) was quilted with straight lines outlining the constellation and an allover clamshell pattern filling in the rest of the quilt.

3. Bind the quilt with the binding strips.

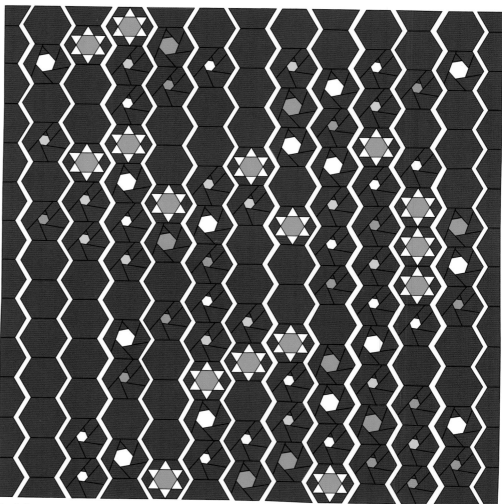

Quilt layout

Stardust and Moonbeams

HEXAGON SIZE: 2" • FINISHED QUILT: 21¼" × 24"

MADE BY Emily Breclaw

The charm of this mini-quilt lies in the irregularity of the tiny pieced singles. Use leftover scraps from *Hello, Orion* (page 65) or any small bits of special fabric.

materials

INDIGO: Scraps to total ⅝ yard (Each scrap should measure about 2¾″ × 1¾″.)

YELLOW: ¼ yard

TAUPE: ½ yard

LIGHT GRAY: ⅝ yard

BORDER: ¼ yard

BACKING: ¾ yard

BINDING: ⅓ yard

BATTING: 26″ × 28″

cutting

Use the 2″ hexagon family of patterns (pages 108 and 109). Refer to Cutting and Preparing Patches (page 7) as needed.

INDIGO

- If using yardage, cut 6 strips 2¾″ × width of fabric; subcut into 114 rectangles, 2¾″ × 1¾″.

  or

- If using scraps, select 114 scraps approximately 1¾″ × 2¾″.

YELLOW

- Cut 1 strip 2¾″ × width of fabric; subcut into 6 rectangles, 2¾″ × 1¾″.

- Cut 1 strip 2¼″ × width of fabric; subcut into 6 triangles.

TAUPE

- Cut 2 strips 4″ × width of fabric; subcut into 9 hexagons.

- Cut 2 strips 2¼″ × width of fabric; subcut into 26 triangles.

LIGHT GRAY

- Cut 5 strips 2¾″ × width of fabric; subcut into 108 rectangles, 2¾″ × 1¾″.

- Cut 2 strips 2¼″ × width of fabric; subcut into 22 triangles.

BORDERS

- Cut 3 strips 2¼″ × width of fabric.

BINDING

- Cut 3 strips 2½″ × width of fabric.

construction

Seam allowances are ¼″. Unless otherwise indicated, do not sew into the seam allowances. Refer to Sewing Hexagons and Related Shapes (page 15) as needed.

Block Assembly

TWIRLY SINGLE

GATHER	Indigo scraps
	Light gray rectangles

1. Sew an indigo scrap or rectangle to a light gray rectangle. (This seam may be sewn edge to edge rather than dot to dot). Press the seam open.

2. Repeat Step 1 with 5 additional indigo rectangles or scraps and the light gray rectangles to make 6 pieced units total.

Using rectangles

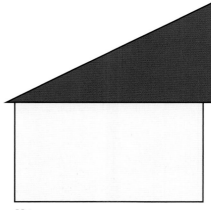

Using scraps

3. Cut each of the 6 pieced units into triangles. Make sure that one side of the triangle is completely indigo. Mark seam dots on the pieced triangles.

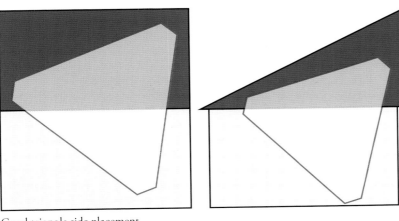
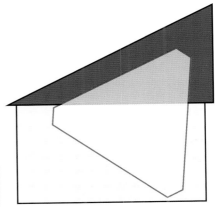

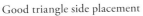

Good triangle side placement

Incorrect triangle side placement. One side must be completely indigo.

4. Arrange the 6 triangles so that all the indigo sides of the triangle start at the center of the block and no indigo side of one triangle is touching an indigo side of another triangle.

5. Sew the triangles dot to dot to form 2 half-hexagons. Press toward the solid indigo side of the triangle.

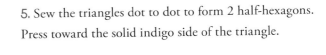

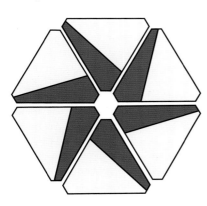

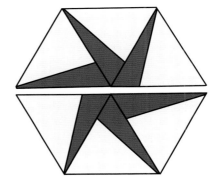

6. Sew the 2 half-hexagons together. Swirl the middle seams to reduce bulk. (See Pressing Units, page 18.)

7. Repeat to make a total of 18 Twirly Singles.

8. Repeat Steps 1–6 with 6 indigo scraps and the 6 yellow rectangles to make 1 Twirly Single in yellow and indigo.

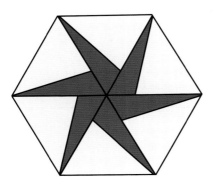

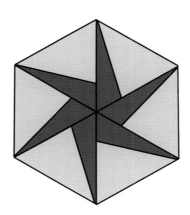

Quilt Assembly

Refer to the quilt layout diagram (next page) while assembling the rows.

1. Arrange the Twirly Singles, triangles, and hexagons on a design wall according to the layout diagram.

2. Sew triangles to 2 sides of each hexagon first. *Note: Four hexagons on the top and bottom of the quilt have 3 triangles sewn to the sides.*

3. Press toward the triangles. *Fig. A*

4. Sew the units from Step 1 into columns. *Fig. B*

TIP ⫶ BLOCK ALIGNMENT

Unlike traditional seams, the seams created when sewing this quilt into columns will not nest. Instead you need to ensure that the seam from the top unit crosses the seam on the bottom unit at exactly the same point as your needle will pass when sewing them together. After you've lined up the edges of 2 units, place a pin exactly through the dot at the center of your seam and make sure it passes through the dot on the other patch. With that pin in place, you can gently pull back on the top patch (as if you're looking into the seam allowance before it's sewn) to be sure the patches will align exactly.

5. Press the seams open.

6. Sew the columns together, keeping in mind the instructions in Tip: Block Alignment (above).

Borders

1. Place the quilt top on a large, flat surface. Trim the top and bottom rows, using a long acrylic ruler and a rotary cutter. Line up the ¼″ marking on the ruler with the intersection of the sewn triangles. When you trim the quilt top, you will have half-triangles and house half-hexagons remaining.

2. Gather the border strips. Refer to Sewing Borders (page 21) to attach the borders to the quilt.

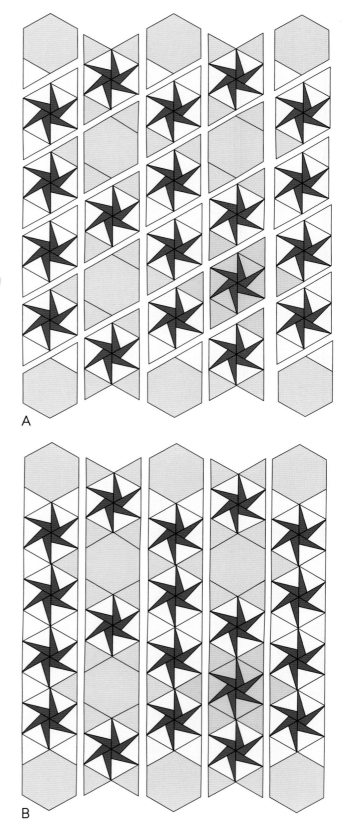

A

B

Finishing

1. Layer the quilt top with the batting and backing. Baste and quilt as desired. The quilt as shown (page 73) was quilted with wavy lines and tiny loops.

2. Bind the quilt with the binding strips.

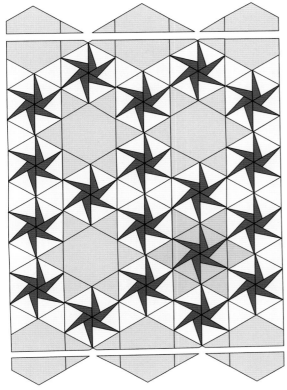

Quilt layout

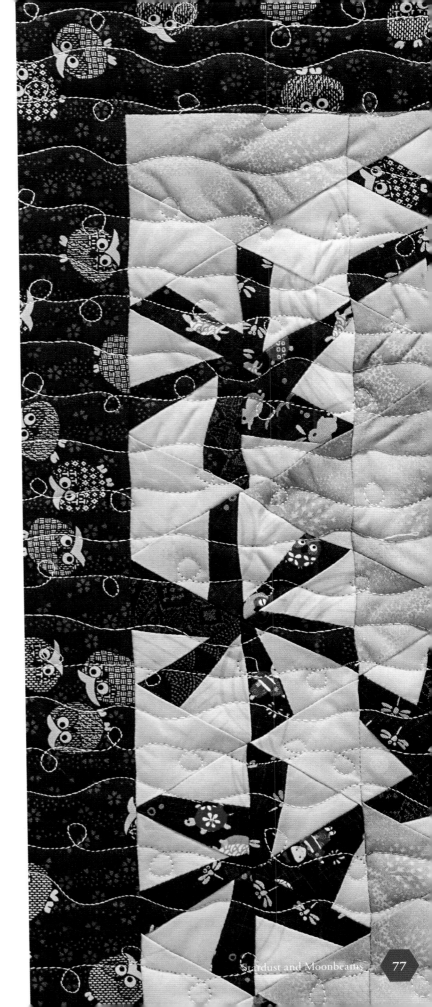

Midsummer Night's Dream

HEXAGON SIZE: 3" • FINISHED QUILT: 87½" × 100"

PIECED BY Emily Breclaw
QUILTED BY Amy Jameson

Fabrics: Handcrafted and Sun Print by Alison Glass for Andover Fabrics

Here's a fantastic opportunity to explore the difference that color and arrangement can make. All the large, bright units are the same pieced medallion, but color choices make each one different. The rosettes surrounding the medallions are identical blocks, with the center rosettes in the inverse color arrangement of the outer rosettes.

materials

NAVY: 7 yards

TURQUOISE: 1⅜ yards

YELLOW: ⅝ yard

ORANGE: ⅜ yard

RED: ½ yard

DARK RED: ⅜ yard

VERY DARK RED: ¼ yard

LAVENDER: ⅜ yard

GRAY: ¼ yard

DARK GRAY: ¼ yard

FUCHSIA: ⅝ yard

TEAL: ¼ yard

LIGHT BLUE: ⅜ yard

DARK BLUE: ⅜ yard

GREEN: ⅜ yard

WHITE: ⅜ yard

BORDERS: 1⅛ yards

BACKING: 3 yards of
108″-wide backing

BINDING: ⅞ yard

BATTING: 94″ × 106″

cutting

Use the 3″ hexagon family of patterns (pages 105–107). In the instructions that follow, large shapes measure 3″ on a side and small shapes measure 1½″ on a side. Refer to Cutting and Preparing Patches (page 7) as needed.

NAVY

- Cut 21 strips 5¾″ × width of fabric; subcut into 121 hexagons.
- Cut 6 strips 3½″ × width of fabric; subcut into 36 house half-hexagons.
- Cut 14 strips 3⅛″ × width of fabric; subcut into 36 large half-hexagons, 36 large diamonds, and 72 large triangles.
- Cut 4 strips 2″ × width of fabric.
- Cut 22 strips 1¹³⁄₁₆″ × width of fabric.
- Cut 3 strips 1¹³⁄₁₆″ × width of fabric; subcut into 48 small diamonds.

TURQUOISE

- Cut 2 strips 2″ × width of fabric.
- Cut 22 strips 1¹³⁄₁₆″ × width of fabric.

YELLOW

- Cut 3 strips 3⅛″ × width of fabric; subcut into 24 large triangles and 6 large half-hexagons.
- Cut 4 strips 2″ × width of fabric.

ORANGE

- Cut 2 strips 3⅛″ × width of fabric; subcut into 12 large diamonds and 12 large triangles.
- Cut 2 strips 2″ × width of fabric.

RED

- Cut 2 strips 3⅛″ × width of fabric; subcut into 6 large triangles and 6 large half-hexagons.
- Cut 4 strips 2″ × width of fabric.

DARK RED

- Cut 2 strips 3⅛″ × width of fabric; subcut into 12 large diamonds and 6 large half-hexagons.

VERY DARK RED

- Cut 1 strip 3⅛″ × width of fabric; subcut into 6 large triangles.

LAVENDER

- Cut 2 strips 3⅛″ × width of fabric; subcut into 6 large diamonds and 6 large triangles.

GRAY

- Cut 1 strip 3⅛″ × width of fabric; subcut into 6 large half-hexagons.

DARK GRAY

- Cut 1 strip 3⅛″ × width of fabric; subcut into 6 large triangles.

FUCHSIA

- Cut 3 strips 3⅛″ × width of fabric; subcut into 12 large diamonds, 6 large triangles, and 6 large half-hexagons.
- Cut 2 strips 2″ × width of fabric.
- Cut 2 strips 1¹³⁄₁₆″ × width of fabric; subcut into 48 small triangles.

TEAL

- Cut 1 strip 3⅛″ × width of fabric; subcut into 6 large triangles.

LIGHT BLUE

- Cut 2 strips 3⅛″ × width of fabric; subcut into 12 large diamonds.

DARK BLUE

- Cut 3 strips 3⅛″ × width of fabric; subcut into 6 large diamonds, 6 large half-hexagons, and 12 large triangles.

GREEN

- Cut 1 strip 3⅛″ × width of fabric; subcut into 6 large triangles.
- Cut 2 strips 2″ × width of fabric.

WHITE

- Cut 2 strip 3⅛″ × width of fabric; subcut into 12 large triangles and 8 small hexagons.

BORDERS

- Cut 9 strips 3½″ × width of fabric.

BINDING

- Cut 10 strips 2½″ × width of fabric.

construction

Seam allowances are ¼". Do not sew into the seam allowances. Refer to Sewing Hexagons and Related Shapes (page 15) as needed.

Block Assembly

NEBULA #1

GATHER			
	2 turquoise 2″ strips	12 large navy diamonds	6 yellow triangles
	2 fuchsia 2″ strips	6 lavender diamonds	6 yellow half-hexagons
	6 teal triangles	12 navy triangles	1 navy hexagon
	6 white triangles		

1. Sew 1 turquoise and 1 fuchsia 2″ strip along both sides, as explained in Cutting Shapes from Pieced Strips (page 9). Repeat with the second pair of turquoise and fuchsia strips. Cut 12 pieced diamonds from the pieced strips. Press the seams open. *Fig. A*

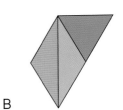

A

2. Sew a teal triangle to 6 of the diamonds from Step 1, paying careful attention to color placement. Press toward the triangles. *Fig. B*

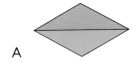

B

3. Sew a white triangle to each of the remaining 6 pieced diamonds. Press toward the triangles. *Fig. C*

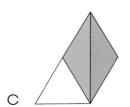

C

4. Sew the units from Step 3 to the units from Step 2. *Fig. D*

TIP ALIGNING TRIANGLE POINTS

It can be tricky to ensure that your triangle points in this unit align perfectly. When you line up the 2 units to pin them, nestle the triangle fabrics between the diamond fabrics in the unsewn seam allowance. This will give you perfect points every time.

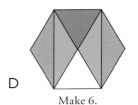

D

Make 6.

5. Sew the 12 navy diamonds into pairs. *Fig. E*

6. Sew a lavender diamond to each pair of navy diamonds from Step 5. *Fig. F*

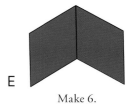

E

Make 6.

F

Make 6.

7. Sew the navy and yellow triangles into groups of 3. *Fig. G*

8. Sew a dark yellow half-hexagon to each unit from Step 7. *Fig. H*

9. Arrange the units around the navy hexagon and sew them into rows. *Fig. I*

10. Sew together the rows to complete the Nebula #1 medallion. *Fig. J*

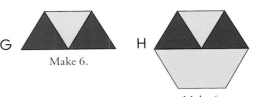

G Make 6.

H Make 6.

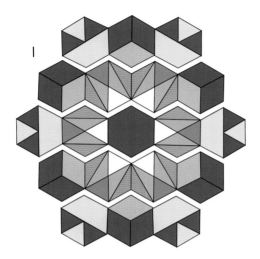

I

J

NEBULA #2

GATHER		
	2 orange 2″ strips	12 dark red diamonds
	2 red 2″ strips	6 orange triangles
	6 yellow triangles	6 navy half-hexagons
	18 navy triangles	1 navy hexagon
	6 navy diamonds	

1. Follow Nebula #1, Steps 1–8 (previous page), changing the colors to match the following diagrams.

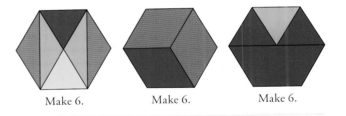

Make 6.

Make 6.

Make 6.

2. Arrange the units around the navy hexagon and sew them into rows.

3. Sew together the rows to complete the Nebula #2 medallion.

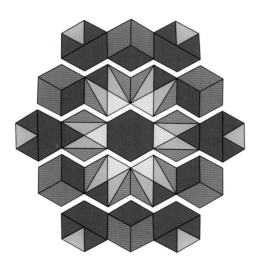

NEBULA #3

GATHER	2 red 2″ strips	6 large navy diamonds
	2 navy 2″ strips	6 very dark red triangles
	6 lavender triangles	12 navy triangles
	6 red triangles	6 dark red half-hexagons
	12 orange diamonds	1 navy hexagon

1. Follow Nebula #1, Steps 1–8 (page 80), changing the colors to match the following diagrams.

Make 6.   Make 6.   Make 6.

2. Arrange the units around the navy hexagon and sew them into rows.

3. Sew together the rows to complete the Nebula #3 medallion.

NEBULA #4

GATHER	2 yellow 2″ strips	6 dark gray triangles
	2 navy 2″ strips	12 navy triangles
	6 green triangles	6 gray half-hexagons
	6 white triangles	7 navy hexagons

1. Follow Nebula #1, Steps 2–4 (page 80) and Steps 7 and 8 (page 81), changing the colors and pieced units to match the following diagrams.

Make 6.   Make 6.

2. Arrange the units and the 7 navy hexagons and sew them into rows.

3. Sew together the rows to complete the Nebula #4 medallion.

NEBULA #5

GATHER		
2 green 2″ strips	6 yellow triangles
2 yellow 2″ strips	12 navy triangles
6 dark blue triangles	6 fuchsia half-hexagons
6 fuchsia triangles	7 navy hexagons

1. Follow Nebula #1, Steps 2–4 (page 80) and Steps 7 and 8 (page 81), changing the colors and pieced units to match the following diagrams.

Make 6.   Make 6.

2. Arrange the units and 7 navy hexagons and sew them into rows.

3. Sew the rows together to complete the Nebula #5 medallion.

NEBULA #6

GATHER		
12 light blue diamonds	6 dark blue diamonds	
6 dark blue triangles	6 red half-hexagons	
6 orange triangles	6 navy half-hexagons	
12 navy diamonds	1 navy hexagon	

1. Follow Nebula #1, Steps 2–6 (page 80) and Step 8 (page 81), changing the colors and pieced units to match the following diagrams.

Make 6. Make 6. Make 6.

2. Arrange the units around the navy hexagon and sew them into rows

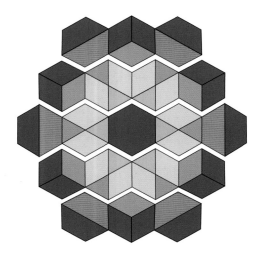

3. Sew together the rows to complete the Nebula #6 medallion.

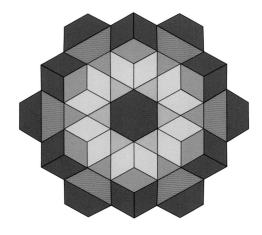

NEBULA #7

GATHER		
12 fuchsia diamonds	6 dark blue half-hexagons	
6 yellow triangles	6 navy half-hexagons	
6 navy triangles	7 navy hexagons	

1. Follow Nebula #1, Steps 2–4 (page 80) and Step 8 (page 81), changing the colors and pieced units to match the following diagrams.

Make 6. Make 6.

2. Arrange the units and 7 navy hexagons and sew them into rows.

3. Sew the rows together to complete the Nebula #7 medallion.

RIBBON ROSETTE

22 navy strips 11³⁄₁₆″	
22 turquoise strips 11³⁄₁₆″	
10 large navy hexagons	

1. Sew a navy strip to each turquoise strip, yielding a total of 22 pieced strip sets. Press the strip sets open.

2. Cut each strip set into 3″ triangles, rotating the template after each cut. *Fig. A*

A

3. Separate the triangles into piles of turquoise points and navy points. You will have about 70 triangles with navy points left over. Save them for another project or use as appliqué accents on the quilt backing. *Fig. B*

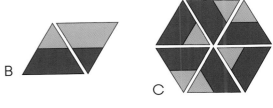

B

C

4. Arrange 6 triangles from the pile with turquoise points. *Fig. C*

5. Sew 4 triangles from Step 4 into pairs. *Fig. D*

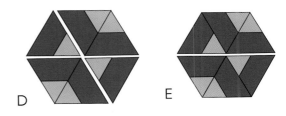

D

E

6. Sew the remaining triangles to the pairs from Step 5. You now have two identical half-hexagons. Press both halves so the seams are going in the same direction. *Fig. E*

7. Join the two halves. Press half the seam up and the other half down so that all the seams swirl around the center. (See Pressing Units, page 18.) *Fig. F*

F

8. Repeat Steps 4–7 to make 5 more units.

9. Arrange the 6 pieced hexagons and 1 solid navy hexagon and sew them into rows.

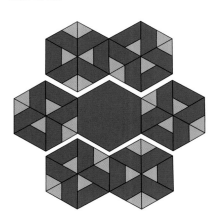

10. Sew rows together to complete the rosette.

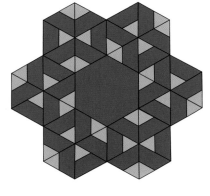

13. Make a total of 4 rosettes with navy points. These will be referred to as the light Ribbon Rosettes.

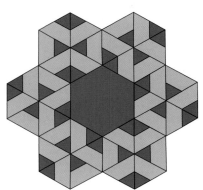

11. Repeat Steps 4–10 to make a total of 6 rosettes. These will be referred to as the dark Ribbon Rosettes.

12. Repeat Steps 4–10 to make rosettes with the triangles with navy points.

STARRY SINGLE

GATHER	8 small white hexagons
	48 small fuchsia triangles
	48 small navy diamonds

1. Follow *Hello, Orion*, Starry Single, Steps 1 and 2 (page 66).

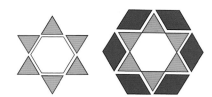

2. Repeat to make a total of 8 Starry Singles.

Quilt Assembly

Refer to the quilt layout diagram (page 89) while assembling the rows. Press the horizontal seams up. Swirl the angled intersections around the horizontal seams. (See Pressing Units, page 18.) To make the quilts as shown, follow the instructions and the quilt layout diagram, but feel free to play with the placement of the Nebula medallions.

1. Sew a Nebula medallion to 2 light Ribbon Rosettes and 2 Starry Singles. Sew 5 navy hexagons as shown and sew each to one side of the row.

2. Sew 2 Nebula medallions, 2 dark Ribbon Rosettes, 1 Starry Single, and 4 navy hexagons as shown.

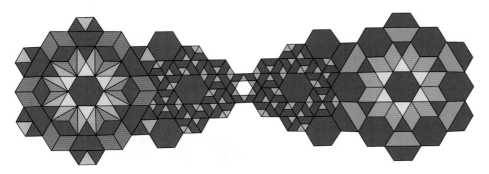

3. Repeat Step 1 to make the center row, but use 2 dark Ribbon Rosettes instead of the light Ribbon Rosettes used in rows 1 and 5.

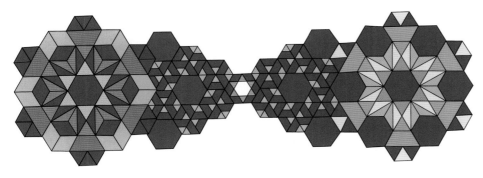

4. Repeat Step 2 to make the fourth row.

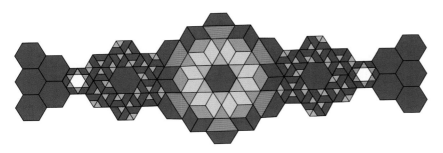

5. Repeat Step 1 to make the final row.

6. Sew together the rows. See pinning tip in *Independence Day*, Quilt Assembly (page 30), to help ensure accuracy when sewing the rows. *Fig. A*

7. Sew 18 navy house half-hexagons into a row. Repeat to make a second row. *Fig. B*

8. Sew the remaining navy hexagons and half-hexagons as shown. Sew the units to the top and bottom of the quilt top. *Fig. C*

9. Sew the rows from Step 7 to each side of the quilt top.

Borders

Gather the border strips. Refer to Sewing Borders (page 21) to attach the borders to the quilt

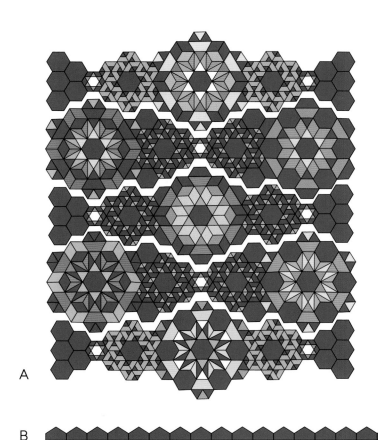

A

B

C

Finishing

1. Layer the quilt top with the batting and backing. Baste and quilt as desired. The quilt as shown (page 78) was quilted with an allover curved crescent pattern.

2. Bind the quilt with the binding strips.

Quilt layout

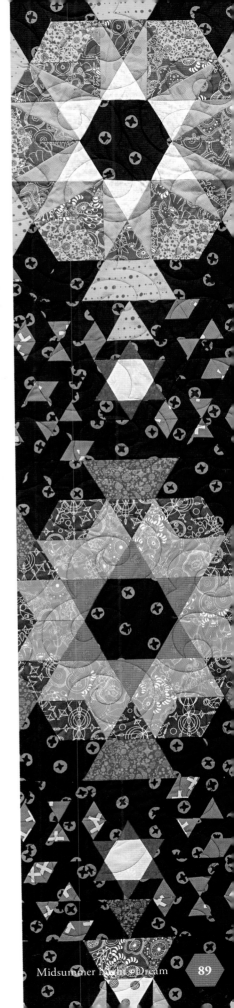

Superstar

HEXAGON SIZE: 3″ • FINISHED QUILT: 68¾″ × 78½″

MADE BY Emily Breclaw

Fabrics: Vintage Japanese yukata

This fun quilt is the magnum opus of the entire book—a crazy quilt made of units from previous projects, plus some unique rosettes, triples, and singles. Make this quilt your own by swapping blocks for your favorites. (For Japanese yukata fabrics, okanarts.com is a good source.)

materials

NAVY: ¾ yard

GOLD: ¾ yard

ORANGE: ⅜ yard

PINK: ½ yard

TEAL: ¼ yard

BLACK: ⅞ yard

RUST: ⅜ yard

LIGHT BLUE: ⅜ yard

PURPLE: ¾ yard

VERY LIGHT TURQUOISE:
⅜ yard

CREAM: ⅛ yard

BLUE: ½ yard

ASSORTED PRINT FABRICS:
2½ yards total for background
hexagons (If using scraps,
be sure each strip is at least
5¾" wide.)

BORDER: ⅞ yard

BACKING: 4¾ yards

BINDING: ⅝ yard

BATTING: 75" × 85"

cutting

Use the 3" hexagon family of patterns (pages 105–107). In the instructions that follow, large shapes measure 3" on a side and small shapes measure 1½" on a side.

NAVY

- Cut 1 strip 5¾" × width of fabric; subcut into 2 large hexagons.
- Cut 4 strips 3⅛" × width of fabric; subcut into 36 large diamonds, 1 large triangle, and 1 large kite.

GOLD

- Cut 1 strips 5¾" × width of fabric; subcut into 6 large hexagons.
- Cut 4 strips 3⅛" × width of fabric; subcut into 24 large diamonds, 13 large triangles, and 1 large kite.
- Cut 1 strip 2" × width of fabric.

ORANGE

- Cut 2 strips 3⅛" × width of fabric; subcut into 13 large triangles, 12 large diamonds, and 1 large kite.
- Cut 2 strips 1¹³⁄₁₆" × width of fabric.

PINK

- Cut 4 strips 3⅛" × width of fabric; subcut into 12 large half-hexagons, 18 large triangles, and 10 small hexagons.

TEAL

- Cut 1 strip 3⅛" × width of fabric; subcut into 6 large half-hexagons, 1 large triangle, and 1 large kite.
- Cut 1 strip 1¹³⁄₁₆" × width of fabric; subcut into 18 small diamonds.

BLACK

- Cut 4 strips 3½" × width of fabric; subcut into 24 house half-hexagons.
- Cut 3 strips 3⅛" × width of fabric; subcut into 16 large half-hexagons.
- Cut 1 strip 2" × width of fabric.

RUST

- Cut 2 strips 3⅛" × width of fabric; subcut into 12 large diamonds.

LIGHT BLUE

- Cut 1 strip 5¾" × width of fabric; subcut into 6 large hexagons.

PURPLE

- Cut 1 strip 5¾" × width of fabric; subcut into 1 large hexagon and 6 large half-hexagons.
- Cut 2 strips 3⅛" × width of fabric; subcut into 12 large diamonds and 6 large triangles.
- Cut 3 strips 1¹³⁄₁₆" × width of fabric; subcut into 42 small diamonds.

VERY LIGHT TURQUOISE

- Cut 1 strip 3⅛" × width of fabric; subcut into 1 large triangle and 1 large kite.
- Cut 3 strips 1¹³⁄₁₆" × width of fabric; subcut into 60 small triangles.

CREAM

- Cut 2 strips 1¹³⁄₁₆" × width of fabric.

BLUE

- Cut 1 strip 5¾" × width of fabric; subcut into 6 large hexagons.
- Cut 1 strip 3⅛" × width of fabric; subcut into 1 large triangle and 1 large kite.

ASSORTED PRINT FABRICS

- Cut 14 strips 5¾" × width of fabric; subcut into 79 large hexagons.

BORDERS

- Cut 8 strips 3½" × width of fabric.

BINDING

- Cut 8 strips 2½" × width of fabric.

construction

Seam allowances are ¼". Do not sew into the seam allowances.
Refer to Sewing Hexagons and Related Shapes (page 15) as needed.

Block Assembly

NEBULA MEDALLION

GATHER		
	1 large purple hexagon	6 large purple diamonds
	6 large pink triangles	12 large orange diamonds
	12 large gold diamonds	6 large pink half-hexagons
	6 large purple triangles	6 large teal half-hexagons

1. Follow *Midsummer Night's Dream*, Nebula #1, Steps 2–6 (page 80) and Step 8 (page 81), changing the colors and pieced units to match the following diagrams.

Make 6.   Make 6.   Make 6.

2. Arrange the units and sew them into rows.

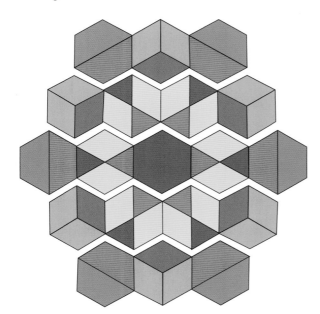

3. Sew rows together to complete the Nebula Medallion.

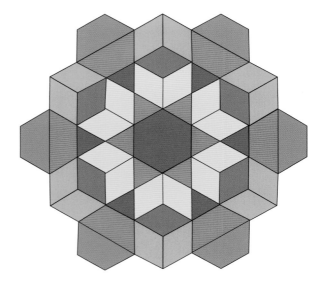

STAR-SPANGLED MEDALLION

GATHER		
	1 large navy hexagon	6 large light blue hexagons
	6 large gold hexagons	12 large pink triangles.
	6 large gold triangles	6 large pink half-hexagons

1. Follow *Independence Day*, Star-Spangled Medallion, Steps 3–7 (page 29), changing the colors and pieced units to match the following diagrams.

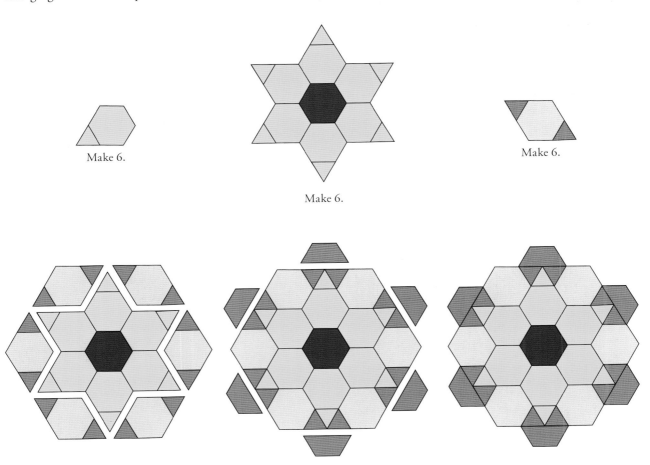

Make 6.

Make 6.

Make 6.

SWIRLING SPROCKET

GATHER	Black and gold 2″ strips	6 large gold triangles
	6 large blue hexagons	12 large gold diamonds

1. Follow *Confetti in Times Square*, Swirling Sprocket, Steps 1–7 (page 39), changing the colors to match the following diagrams.

Make 6.

Make 6.

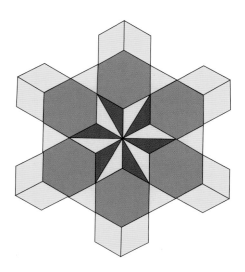

TWO-TONE ROSETTE

GATHER	1 large navy hexagon	12 large orange triangles.
	12 large navy diamonds	

1. Follow *Starburst*, Sunshine Rosette, Steps 1–4 (page 55), changing the colors to match the following diagrams.

Make 12.

Make 6.

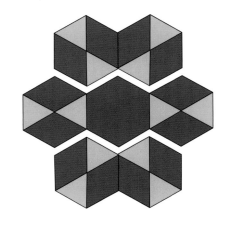

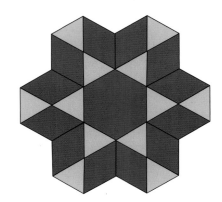

HEXAGON PUZZLE ROSETTE

GATHER	6 large purple diamonds	1 large orange triangle
	6 large purple half-hexagons	1 large navy kite
	1 large very light turquoise kite	1 large navy triangle
	1 large very light turquoise triangle	1 large gold kite
	1 large teal kite	1 large gold triangle
	1 large teal triangle	1 large blue kite
	1 large orange kite	1 large blue triangle

1. Sew the 6 large kites into two groups of three. Sew the two groups into a hexagon. Swirl the seams clockwise around the center. (See Pressing Units, page 18.)

2. Sew triangles to the sides of the unit from Step 1. Pay careful attention to the color arrangement.

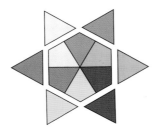

3. Sew purple diamonds between the triangles from Step 2.

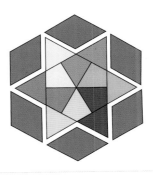

4. Sew a purple half-hexagon to each side of the unit from Step 3.

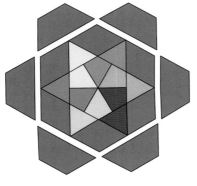

5. Press toward the half-hexagons.

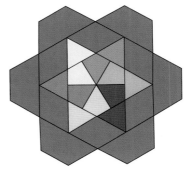

DIAMOND STAR TRIPLE

GATHER	24 large navy diamonds
	12 large rust diamonds

1. Follow *Loverly*, Diamond Star Single, Steps 1 and 2 (page 24), changing the colors to match the following diagrams.

2. Repeat Step 1 to make a total of 4 Diamond Star Triples.

Make 3.

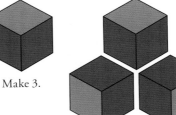

COG SINGLE

GATHER

3 small pink hexagons

18 small teal diamonds

18 small very light turquoise triangles

1. Sew a small very light turquoise triangle to a small teal diamond. Repeat to make a total of 6 units.

Make 6.

2. Sew the units from Step 1 to the sides of the pink hexagon.

3. Repeat Steps 1 and 2 to make a total of 3 Cog Singles.

ORIGAMI SINGLE

GATHER

2 orange 1¹³⁄₁₆″ strips

2 cream 1¹³⁄₁₆″ strips

1. Follow *Midsummer Night's Dream*, Ribbon Rosette, Steps 1–7 (page 85), changing the colors *and* the direction of the triangles to match the following diagrams.

Make 18 of each.

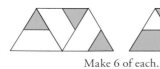

Make 6 of each.

2. Make a total of 3 Origami Singles with orange points and 3 Origami Singles with cream points.

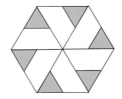 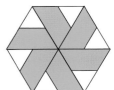

STARRY SINGLE

GATHER

7 small pink hexagons

42 small very light turquoise triangles

42 small purple diamonds

1. Follow *Starburst*, Starry Single, Steps 1 and 2 (page 56), changing the colors to match the following diagrams.

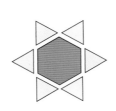 

2. Repeat Step 1 to make a total of 7 Starry Singles.

Quilt Assembly

Refer to the quilt layout diagram (page 99) while assembling the rows. Press the vertical seams to the right. Swirl the remaining seams around the vertical seams. (See Pressing Units, page 18.)

For this section you will need the remaining large hexagons, the black half-hexagons, and the black house half-hexagons.

1. Sew 12 large house half-hexagons in a row along the short sides, as shown.
Repeat to make a second row.

2. Sew 1 Diamond Star Triple, 1 Starry Single, 1 Origami Single, 2 Cog Singles, 16 large assorted hexagons, and 2 house half-hexagons together as shown.

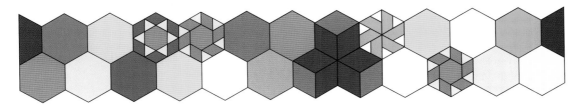

3. Sew the Star-Spangled Medallion, the Swirling Sprocket, 3 Starry Singles, 1 Origami Single, 21 assorted large hexagons, and 6 black half-hexagons together as shown.

4. Sew the Two-Tone Rosette, the Hexagon Puzzle Rosette, 3 Origami Singles, 2 Starry Singles, 1 Cog Single, 21 assorted large hexagons, and 4 black half-hexagons together as shown to create the left half.

5. Sew the Nebula Medallion, 2 Diamond Star Triples, 1 Origami Single, 1 Starry Single, 21 assorted large hexagons, and 4 black half-hexagons together as shown to create the right half.

6. Sew the unit from Step 4 to the unit from Step 5.

7. Sew the unit from Step 2 to the unit from Step 3.

8. Sew the unit from Step 7 to the unit from Step 6.

9. Sew the rows of house half-hexagons to the top and bottom of the quilt.

10. Trim the sections of the house half-hexagons that extend beyond the sides of the quilt top flush with the rest of the top.

Borders

Gather the border strips. Refer to Sewing Borders (page 21) to attach the borders to the quilt.

Finishing

1. Cut the backing in half to get 2 pieces, each approximately 40″ by 85″. Trim the selvages. Sew the 2 pieces, right sides together, along an 85″ side. Press the seam.

2. Layer the quilt top with the batting and backing. Baste and quilt as desired. The quilt as shown (page 90) was quilted with wavy spirals in the large blocks, and a meandering spiral design over the rest of the quilt.

3. Bind the quilt with the binding strips.

Quilt layout

Design Primer

All the quilt projects in this book are presented with an ulterior motive—to serve as a springboard for your creativity. Every block in this book, from medallions down to singles, can fit together in the same quilt. Now it's time to explore some what-if possibilities.

exploring design options

What if you swapped out the rosettes and singles in *Starburst* (page 53) with the Two-Tone Rosette and Origami Single from *Superstar* (page 90)?

What if you traded the medallions from *Independence Day* (page 27) with the medallions and options from *Midsummer Night's Dream* (page 78)?

What if you wanted to combine your own selection of blocks into a spectacular hexagon quilt? With a little advance planning, it is easy to design your own hexagon quilts. First you need to determine the scale of your quilt. The 3″ hexagon family used throughout this book is great for bed-size quilts. The smaller 2″ hexagon family works well for wallhangings or more intricate quilts. The design grids (pages 103 and 104) provide estimates for baby, lap, twin, and queen-size quilts, using the 3″ hexagon family. When I'm designing a quilt, I like to color in the hexagons with different colors for the block types, for example, one color for medallions, another for sprockets, and so on.

Let's take a closer look at this process. Say you're designing a lap-size quilt. Start with the lap design page.

Add a couple of medallions, shown in blue. That fills up a good bit of the quilt space, but there's still room for a few rosettes, shown in green. Lastly, use some triples, shown in orange, to break up any remaining big spaces.

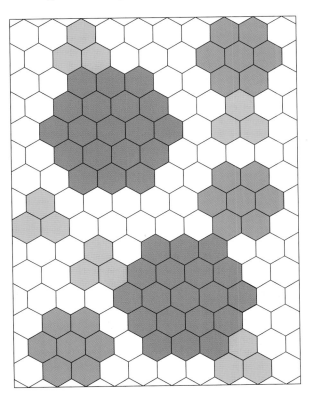

Now you have a map for laying out blocks, and you know that you need to fill in the remaining spots with 69 singles and plain 3″ hexagons, plus half-hexagons at the edges.

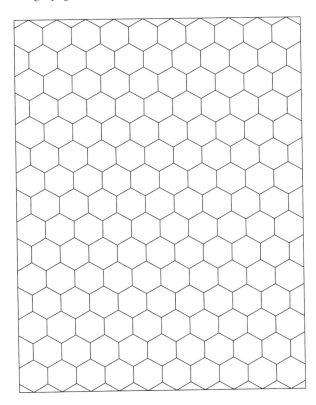

figuring yardage

Going back to the blocks in the projects, you can quickly determine how many shapes you need for each of your blocks. The following table shows patch yields for strips of 40″-wide fabric. Depending on whether you fold your strips before cutting or use bigger English paper piecing seam allowances, you may get slightly different yields. Use the notes section of the table to jot down your yields if they differ from those shown, to provide a handy reference for your future projects.

	Size	Strip width	Yield	Notes
3″ family	3″ hexagon	5¾″	6	
	3″ house half-hexagon	3½″	7	
	3″ half-hexagon	3⅛″	7	
	3″ diamond	3⅛″	10	
	3″ third	3⅛″	7	
	3″ triangle	3⅛″	19	
	3″ kite	2¹³⁄₁₆″	16	
	1½″ hexagon	3⅛″	11	
	1½″ half-hexagon	1¹³⁄₁₆″	13	
	1½″ diamond	1¹³⁄₁₆″	18	
	1½″ triangle	1¹³⁄₁₆″	28	
	¾″ hexagon	1¹³⁄₁₆″	18	
2″ family	2″ hexagon	4″	8	
	2″ house half-hexagon	2½″	10	
	2″ half hexagon	2¼″	10	
	2″ diamond	2¼″	14	
	2″ third	2¼″	10	
	2″ triangle	2¼″	23	
	2″ kite	2⅛″	20	
	1″ hexagon	2¼″	15	
	1″ jewel	2¼″	15	
	1″ half-hexagon	1⅜″	18	
	1″ diamond	1⅜″	24	
	1″ triangle	1⅜″	34	

From the strip yields, you can figure out how much fabric you need.

EXAMPLE

For example, let's say you need 64 triangles that are 3″ for your project. Looking at the table, you know you can get 19 triangles from a 3⅛″ strip.

64 patches needed ÷ 19 patches per strip = 3.36

3.36 rounds up to 4 strips total

To determine the yardage for these strips:

4 strips × 3.125″ (decimal equivalent of 3⅛) = 12.5″

⅜ yard = 13.5″

So that is the minimum needed, or round up to ½ yard (18″) of fabric for the strips.

fabric choices

As you are planning your own hexagon quilts, keep a couple of thoughts in mind about fabric choices. If you skim through this book, you can see most of the background fabrics are not solid; they have a subtle but random pattern. I chose these fabrics intentionally. Sometimes, especially with lots of plain hexagon background blocks, you will have a bit of fullness in the plain patches compared with the pieced ones. Mottled background fabrics will help hide this fullness or any tiny tucks that may occur. For these same reasons, I also chose most of my border fabrics to match or coordinate with the backgrounds.

borders

Finally, piece your borders carefully to accommodate any fullness in the piecing. I included specific steps in Sewing Borders (page 21) for measuring three times, in three different places, on each dimension and cutting border strips to size because this method helps tremendously when it comes to squaring up your quilt. Carefully sewn borders will add a final element of awesomeness to your hexagon masterpieces—and make your longarm quilter's job easier, too.

Now you're all set to create your own amazing hexagon quilts. Happy stitching!

design grids

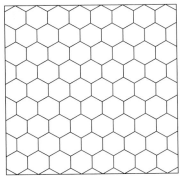

Baby-size, 3″ hexagon 42″ × 42″

Lap-size, 3″ hexagon 52″ × 69″

Twin-size, 3″ hexagon 83″ × 105″

Queen-size, 3″ hexagon 104″ × 114″

Patterns

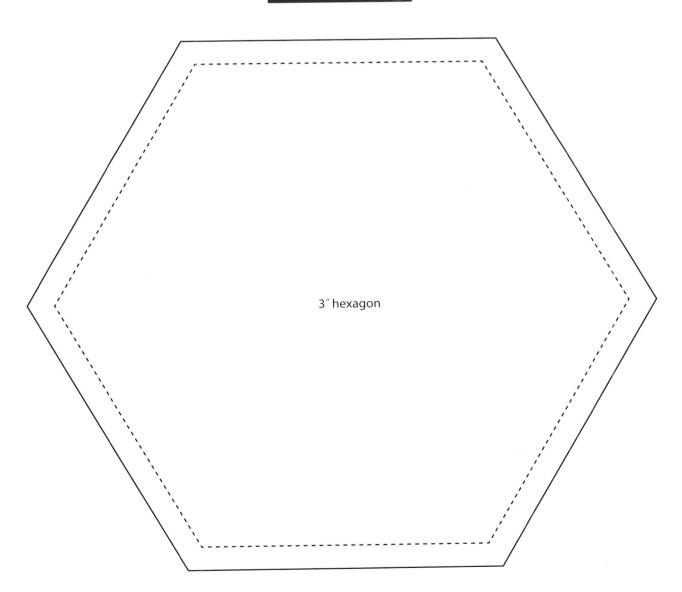

3″ hexagon

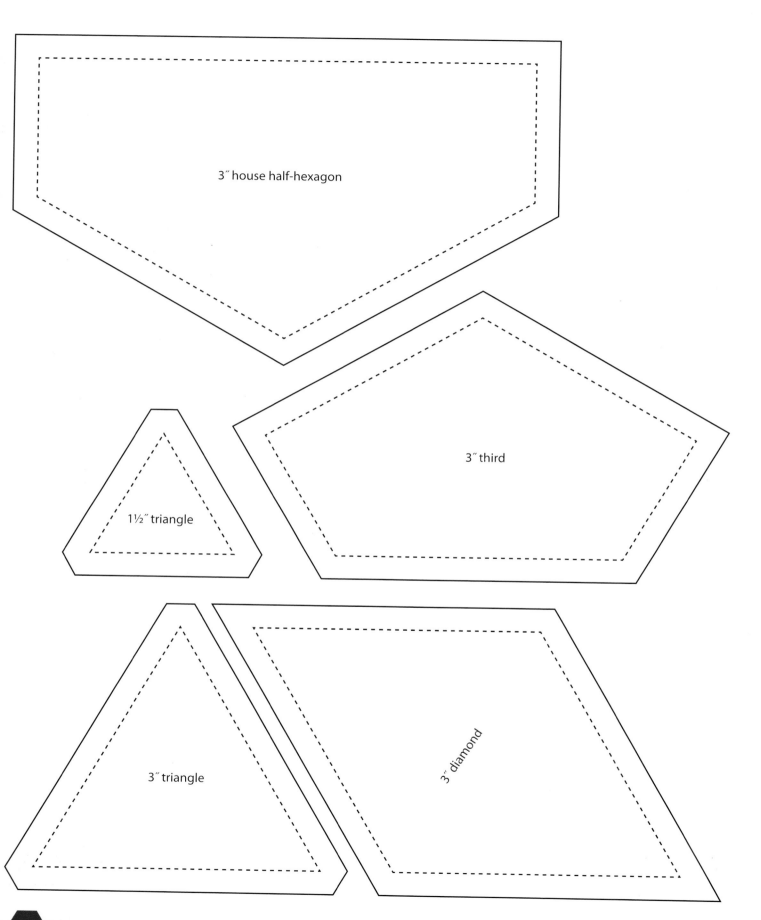

3″ house half-hexagon

1½″ triangle

3″ third

3″ triangle

3″ diamond

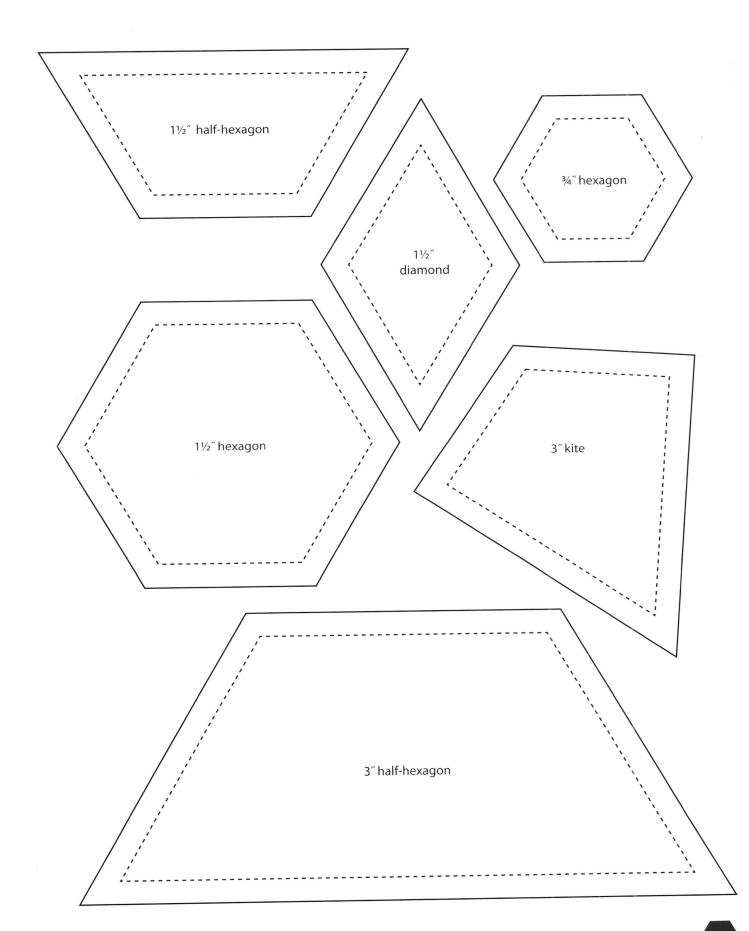

1½˝ half-hexagon

¾˝ hexagon

1½˝ diamond

1½˝ hexagon

3˝ kite

3˝ half-hexagon

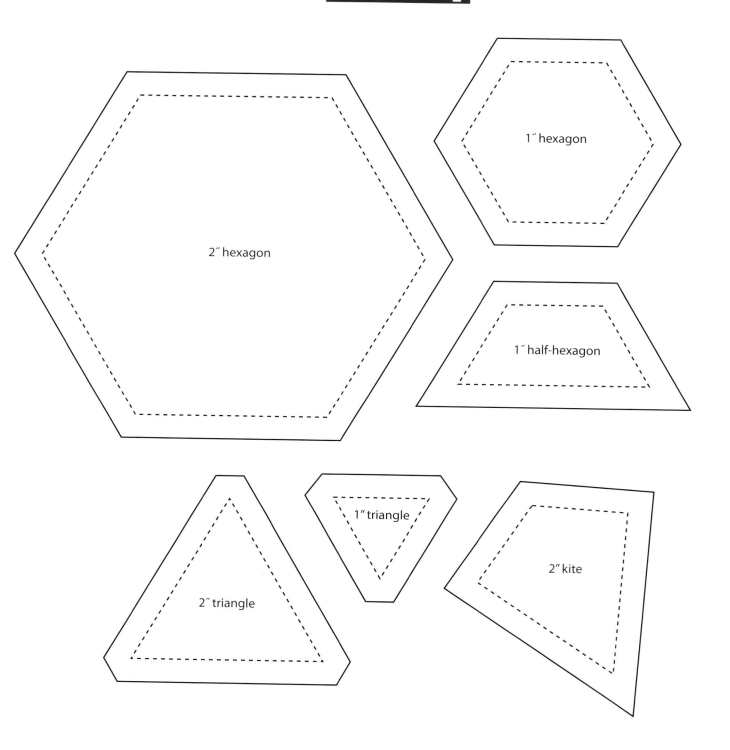

2˝ family

2˝ hexagon

1˝ hexagon

1˝ half-hexagon

2˝ triangle

1" triangle

2" kite

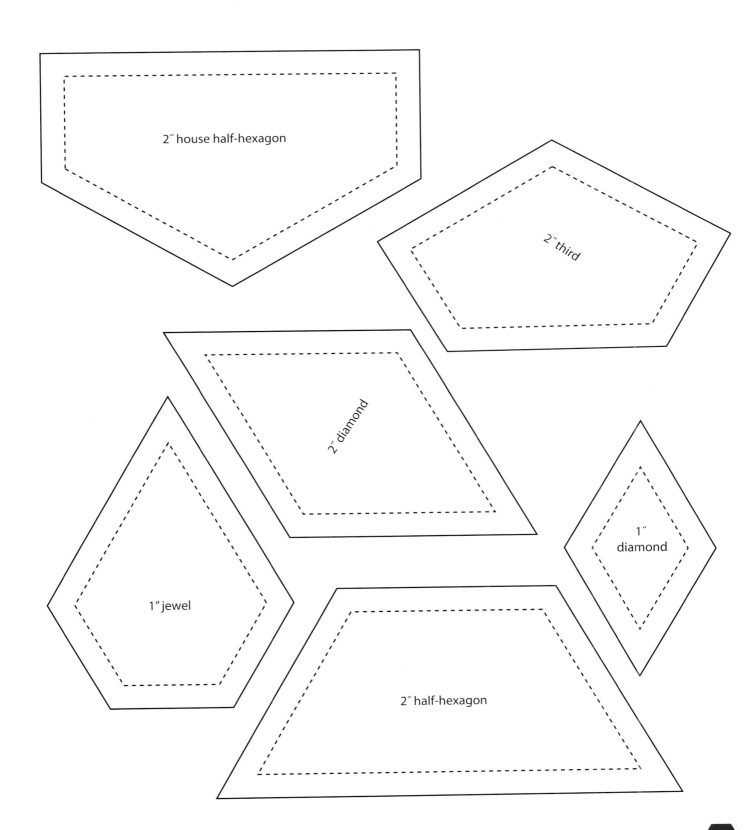

2″ house half-hexagon

2″ third

2″ diamond

1″ diamond

1″ jewel

2″ half-hexagon

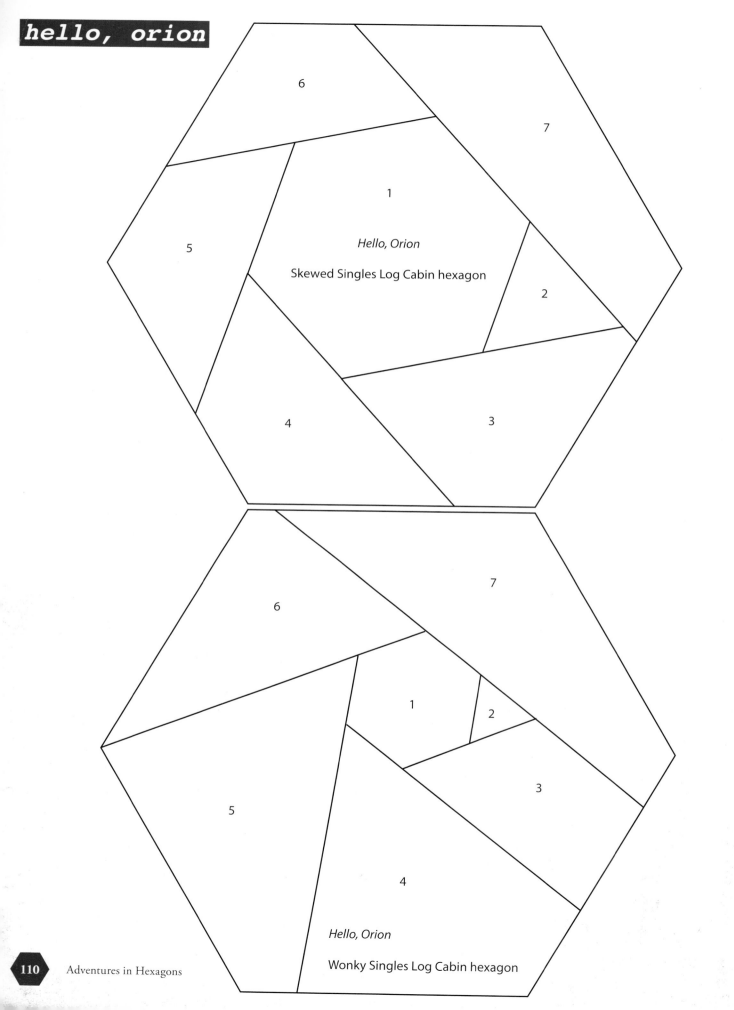

hello, orion

6

7

1

5

Hello, Orion

Skewed Singles Log Cabin hexagon

2

4

3

6

7

1

2

5

3

4

Hello, Orion

Wonky Singles Log Cabin hexagon

About the Author

Emily Breclaw is a quilt designer with a background totally unrelated to anything quilty. She holds a bachelor of science degree in Wildlife and Fisheries Sciences and a master of science in Recreation, Park, and Tourism Sciences. She taught teachers how to use the outdoors as a classroom until the birth of her first child. She started her pattern company, The Caffeinated Quilter, to help quilters expand their skills and discover the addicting fun of hexagon quilt patterns.

Emily's designs have been featured in *Stitch*, *Quiltmaker*, and *American Quilter* magazines. You can follow along with her madcap quilting adventures (and misadventures) at thecaffeinatedquilter.com.

When she's not creating in her studio, Emily enjoys spending time outdoors with her five kids, catching up with friends over coffee, and playing board games with her husband.